M000215036

LAKE
EFFECT

A Deckhand's Journey
On the Great Lakes Freighters

By Richard Hill

LAKE EFFECT

A Deckhand's Journey
On the Great Lakes Freighters

By Richard Hill

Edited by Nancy Steinhaus

Published by
Gale Force Press
Sault Ste. Marie, Michigan

Layout and Design
Globe Printing, Inc., Ishpeming, Michigan
www.globeprinting.net

ISBN # 978-0-9817371-8-8
Library of Congress Control Number: 2008903494

First Printing 2008

Copyright © 2008 Richard Hill
Printed in the United States

All Rights Reserved. No portion of this publication may be
reproduced, reprinted, or otherwise copied for distribution
purposes without express written permission of the author.

Cover Photo Courtesy of the Photographer, Fred Hill
Title Page Painting Courtesy of Mike Wirtanen

To my wife, Judy, and my sons, Travis and Coleman

Acknowledgments

In my efforts to tell this story of my experiences on the lake freighters, I am grateful to a number of individuals. First I am thankful to Nancy Steinhaus for her deft editing skills and her great sense of narrative flow. My appreciation to Bernie Arbic and the Chippewa County Historical Society for helping me locate various old boat photos. I would also like to acknowledge John Wellington for helping to clarify some winter navigation details and Carmen Paris for supplying a few special freighter pictures. For allowing me to browse his extensive collection of Great Lakes freighter photos, special thanks to Fred Hill. I would also like to mention Dennis Dougherty for material for the cover design, and Jim Hill for his early reading of the manuscript and for his helpful suggestions. For the cover design and the interior book layout, I am especially grateful to Stacey Willey and her Globe Printing staff. She has been very supportive and encouraging the entire way. And lastly, thanks go to Max, my cocker spaniel, who slept contentedly on a chair next to me while I wrote, waiting patiently for his daily walk.

Great Lakes Ports

Two Harbors
Duluth
Isle Royale
SUPERIOR
Marquette
Whitefish Point
Escanaba
Chicago
MICHIGAN
Gary
Traverse City
Sault Ste. Marie
Detroit
Toledo
Port Huron
HURON
Lorain
ERIE
Conneaut
ONTARIO

Table of Contents

Introduction

In the late 1960s and early 1970s, I joined many of my friends and all three of my brothers in working on the Great Lakes freighters—"the boats" as we called them. Some of us worked for college money, and others used the boats for short-term employment while deciding what to do with our lives. At the time, the work was plentiful, and we could always find a boat in need of a deckhand. The younger guys worked for several months, earned a few bucks to tide them over, then hopped off for a little shore time. Whenever a few of us boaters got together over the winter, the stories flew back and forth for hours. We still tell them today.

I grew up in Sault Ste. Marie, near the St. Mary's River, and the freighters have always been a part of the culture around me. Generations of locals have worked on the boats, and those of us who live on the river see freighters coming and going through much of the year. Quite often we photograph them for the memories.

To many of us there has always been an element of romance and adventure about the boats as they pass through the Soo Locks, a certain mystery unlike anything else. I grew up with the sound of boat whistles. Books by Melville and Conrad piqued my curiosity about the sailing life and all the unsavory characters I might meet if I was lucky enough to ship out on a steamboat. The day finally came. After the U.S. Coast Guard documented and fingerprinted me, I obtained my Z-card (Merchant Marine Document), my ticket to a good-paying job and an unexpected adventure on the boats.

After working on the steamboats for several years, I left to marry and start a business. But I could not put aside my thoughts of going back to the sailing life. Some years later I enrolled in the Maritime Academy with plans to make a career as a ship's officer on a Great Lakes freighter. As it turned out, the boats and the life I had known in my earlier years had disappeared by that time. I had moved on as well. For several years I thought about telling this story, but life and work always got in the way. Finally the time seemed right.

I currently live on Lake Superior, a few miles upriver from the Soo Locks. Many nights, the last thing I see out my bedroom window is the silhouette of a freighter sliding by out in the bay, trimmed with a string of small yellow lights. Occasionally, if I am lucky, the captain toots his whistle to say hello to someone nearby. I close my eyes and drift away. From a distance, sailing on the freighters still looms as a romantic calling. But only from a distance.

Stirrings

The early morning mist hovered over the quiet waters of the St. Mary's River, slightly obscuring the passing freighters. The rocks along the bank where I sat felt damp and mossy. Further down the river, in the narrow channel, the ferry sounded a muffled horn blast as it departed for Sugar Island. Along the Canadian side of the river, the sugar maples blushed as they awoke in the chill fall air. I had come down to the water with my coffee thermos and my *Free Press* to catch up on the news and enjoy a few quiet moments. I read about the Iraq War that seemed to drag on forever as well as the surging Tigers hot in pursuit of a division championship. There was complete stillness but for the Canada geese foraging in the nearby grass and a thousand-foot freighter, the *Columbia Star,* steaming silently down the river. But, soon enough, several cars showed up and out popped the tourists with their brimmed hats, sunglasses, and telephoto digital cameras. They were on a mission and did not want to miss any of the action. They quickly went to work setting up their tripods and equipment, kindly ignoring my newspaper and me. The buzz of activity began to remind me of a Hollywood set as the giant freighter churned closer towards us. Mission Point, just a mile below the Soo Locks, is one of the narrowest points in the river channel; it's hard to believe that a ship of such mammoth size could squeeze through this tight of an opening. Of course, it's also a photographer's dream location.

The shoreside perspective, or landlubber's view, of life on a Great Lakes freighter has always been a bit too romanticized. Tourists from all parts of the world who visit the area imagine that sailing on these vessels must be a very gallant and noble way of earning a living in today's world. Those devil-may-care sailors must lead very exciting lives traversing the bold blue waters of the Great Lakes, in and out of new ports every week. Not a care in the world. What a great life! Or so it seems.

A tourist shouted out to a deckhand, "Hey! What are you carrying?"

"Iron ore," the deckhand yelled back. "Where are you headed?" asked the tourist. "South Chicago." This exchange would never occur at an airport or a train station. The captain or conductor would never get asked about his inventory or his destination. But here, it's quite common.

Thirty-some years ago, I worked on several U.S. Steel freighters as a deckhand and deckwatch. Back then, U.S. Steel could proudly boast about their fleet of fifty Great Lakes vessels. Whether a college student or a guy down on his luck, a fellow could find work on the freighters quite easily. All one needed was a Merchant Marine Document from the Coast Guard and a little persistence down at Tom Craig's fleet office on the river—that and a sea bag packed and ready to go; a call would usually come with only two or three hours notice, sometimes in the middle of the night. The freighters ran from daylight to dusk and all night long as well, stopping only to load or unload the cargo. The money was good, and room and board was free. It was a great place to save a few dollars for those who could handle the lifestyle.

⚓ ⚓ ⚓

As a kid growing up in Sault Ste. Marie, or "the Soo" as locals call it, back in the '60s and '70s, the Great Lakes freighters held a fascination for me like none other. My friends and I watched them sail up and down the St. Mary's River hauling their cargoes of coal, limestone, and iron ore from exotic ports like Duluth, Two Harbors, and Silver Bay. They were bound for even more mysterious places like Conneaut, Toledo, and South Chicago. For entertainment, we hung around the Soo Locks in the summertime watching the giant ore boats as they were raised or lowered through the MacArthur and the Poe Locks. From a close-up view, we admired the surly looks and the windburned faces of the hulking deckhands. They led a life, no doubt, that was way beyond our humdrum existence. What was it like, we wondered, to be part of a ship's crew and sail into the open blue waters of the Great Lakes? We envied the deckhands' swagger as they nonchalantly went about their duties.

When I graduated from high school in 1970, I wasn't quite sure what I wanted to do next. School had been mentally exhausting for me. Even though I had done well gradewise, I wasn't ready to dive into a college curriculum. The Vietnam War was still dragging on endlessly, and the country had just survived a decade of incredible turbulence. On many college campuses and in several major cities, there were war protests, draft card burnings, and riots, as well as confrontations with the Black Panthers, the Weathermen, and the Chicago Seven. We had lost President Kennedy, Martin Luther King, Jr., and Robert Kennedy to assassination. Hippies and the counterculture movement questioned our values as a nation and our identities as individuals. It seemed as though the entire country had been turned inside out and was searching for new directions.

As soon as school ended, I hitchhiked out to Boston and lived with friends for a few months. I found a job working in the kitchen of the New England Medical Center cafeteria. When I returned to the Soo, I quickly found an apartment so I could be on my own. I, too, was searching for a new course, a new direction to head in. The following summer, my friends and I waited anxiously to see what our draft numbers would be in the lottery. The Army hadn't been sending as many draftees to Vietnam as they had done earlier, but one could never be too sure. I didn't believe in the war. The United States had been propping up a corrupt dictator in South Vietnam and had sacrificed countless American lives for the sake of stopping the advance of communism. Our country was mired in a deep black hole and couldn't seem to find a way out. Our involvement was slowly tearing our country apart. I filed as a conscientious objector with the local draft board but was turned down. The draft in 1971 went as high as number 95; two of my friends were drafted. I was the lucky one with number 125.

After a two-year breather, I was ready to head back to school and applied to the University of Michigan in Ann Arbor. My goal was to become a short-story writer. I wanted to write about people in my life, events, and ideas that meant something to me. Instead of simply finding a good-paying job, I needed to understand the world around me and try to put it into words. The degree didn't interest me as much as the opportunity to take as many English and writing courses as possible. Meanwhile, to finance this scheme, I would need to find a job on the freighters as soon as possible. My brothers had followed this plan successfully by working several summers between college years. With my newly acquired Merchant Marine Document from the Coast Guard, my next job was to find a ship. Every week in October, I found myself down at the waterfront office of Tom Craig, the fellow in charge of hiring seamen through the Great Lakes Fleet warehouse. Slouching behind his desk, his glasses propped on the end of his nose, he would gruffly warn, "Look, I've got a list of over a hundred guys ahead of you. I have to hire them out first before I ever get to your name." So I'd leave his office and gently pester him again the following week. Finally, the call came from Craig: "Be down at the dock with your bags by 9:00 tonight; you're a deckhand on the *Leon Fraser.* And don't be late."

Making Headway

On a cool October night, I climbed aboard the supply boat *Ojibway*. We cruised slowly out to the middle of the darkened St. Mary's River to rendezvous with the approaching freighter, just now departing the Soo Locks downbound. Looking back wistfully at the twinkling lights on shore, I wondered what I was getting myself into. Would I be able to adapt to working on the boats with thirty guys from who knows where? At a hundred and forty-one pounds, was I a burly enough hunk to fit in with this gang of roughnecks? No matter, it was too late to worry now.

The *Ojibway* pulled alongside the moving freighter, and someone lowered a wooden ladder down from ten feet above. The deckhand I was replacing scrambled down, and I, bound securely in my life jacket, grabbed the rungs with a death grip and quickly ascended. The supply boat finished offloading the food and supplies, tooted its horn, and pulled away into the night.

Nervous and unsure of what to do next, I stood off to the side and out of the way while the bosun (short for boatswain) and deckhands sorted the boxes and five-gallon paint cans. "C'mon you assholes," the bosun yelled, "Take your hands out of your pants and get this shit put away." The deckhands mumbled under their breath and went routinely about their work.

I was taken to the forward end of the boat and shown my bunk in a cabin one deck below. Art, a friend from the Soo who would be sharing the room with me, had been working on the *Fraser* since fit-out in April seven months earlier. After a few days, he told me that "the boats" were really getting to him, that he was going a little crazy lately and was afraid that maybe his mind was beginning to slip. Art said he had really wanted to stay on board until layup in December or January, but now he wasn't so sure. The boats, he said, had a curious way of affecting a guy's sanity.

At seven the next morning, the deckwatch woke us for breakfast. Just before eight, I joined the other two deckhands, deckwatch, and watchman on the main deck. The bosun, who some called Dirty Dan behind his back, would assign our work for the day. When I walked out on deck that morning, the other guys checked out the way the new guy was dressed and started to snicker. Most of them wore navy blue watch caps pulled down to their eyebrows but above

Leon Fraser, downbound at the Soo, 1981. (Courtesy of the photographer, Fred Hill)

their ears. They dressed in brown Carhartt canvas coats and nylon insulated windbreakers that were spattered with white cabin paint and various colors of red deck paint. They wore weathered canvas gloves and torn blue jeans with their battered leather work boots. I, on the other hand, was fresh out of J.C. Penney's catalog. Since I didn't own any such work clothes, I had started from scratch. Stiff new blue jeans, pullover sweater with a collared shirt, white high-top Converse gym shoes, and a brand new pair of canvas work gloves. And not a spot of paint on me. I looked as if I were headed to my first day of classes on a college campus. Just then, the bosun swung out of his room, took one glance at me and sneered, "Jumpin' Jesus! What the hell do we got here?" The bosun was a stocky sunburned fellow somewhere in his late thirties or early forties. He had ball bearing eyes and chewed a worn-out toothpick that hung from his lower lip. With a look of disgust, he sniffed and spat over the railing. I swallowed hard and tried to ignore the comments. The bosun went below to the paint locker.

The *Fraser* had locked through at the Soo at nine the night before; our ship was now in the middle of northern Lake Michigan. I took in my first view from the deck of a Great Lakes freighter. What an incredible sight! No land was visible in any direction. The blue-green water and soft rolling waves stretched to the horizon this crisp fall day. Warmed by a brilliant morning sun, the mid-forties temperature was slowly on the rise. A few seagulls soared lazily overhead, waiting for some breakfast scraps to be thrown overboard.

The bosun wanted us to start chipping and painting the coamings on hatches number eleven and twelve. We grabbed our scrapers and went right to work. But it was difficult to focus on the work with all this magnificent scenery around me. I wanted to run back to my cabin, grab the camera, and line everyone up for pictures. Maybe they would want a copy. "Quit playin' with yourself and get some work done." The bosun had appeared from nowhere. I put my head down and started scraping the steel coamings furiously. I couldn't afford to daydream.

Out on the open lakes, the deckhands always worked the day shift from eight to four, doing whatever maintenance was necessary. A deckwatch and a watchman often worked with the deck crew when they weren't busy with their other duties. The *Leon Fraser* was a straight-decker; that is, it had forward and aft cabins separated by three cargo holds and eighteen hatches. She was owned and operated by the U.S. Steel Company in Pittsburgh for the Great Lakes Fleet and measured 640 feet long, 67 feet at the beam, and could carry about 18,000 tons of cargo. She was one of the five "super ships" built in 1942 to help supply steel to the lower lake factories for the war effort.

One of the first crew members I met was a watchman who was known as Crazy Dog. He looked to be in his late forties and had been sailing on the lakes for longer than he wanted to admit. He had a ruddy, weathered complexion and a happy-go-lucky grin that stretched from east to west. Always in a good mood, Crazy Dog seemed to enjoy life whether it was raining or shining. The only guy who could rattle him was the bosun, who liked to sneak up behind him and goose him between the cheeks. One of his hobbies was raising sea monkeys, colorful little seahorselike creatures that he kept in a small aquarium filled with water. Everyone teased him about it, but he didn't mind. He also passed many long hours playing his chromatic harmonica, though we could never quite recognize what tune he was blowing. When it was time to work, he went about his business with gusto and enthusiasm, but not usually in any big hurry. No doubt about it—he danced to a different drummer, with moves I hadn't seen before.

We were headed for South Chicago with a load of iron ore. At two in the morning, about an hour out of port, Red, the deckwatch, roused the deckhands to go to work. "Grab your rain gear," he said, "It's pretty shitty out there." We pulled on our rubber work boots, bulky yellow rain pants, oversized raincoats, and hardhats. It all smelled like ripe gym shoes with a good dose of mildew. The gear kept us dry, but we sweated heavily under the many layers as a result. Out on deck, a cold steady drizzle welcomed us to the Windy City.

Our first job was to unscrew the many hundreds of clamps on the eighteen hatch covers. With about eighty or ninety clamps per hatch, I figured this was going to take the better part of two hours to accomplish. "Move your asses, girls," said the bosun, "I want these sonofabitches off in thirty minutes." As the boat steamed closer towards the city lights, we moved silently in the dark, working from port to starboard between the hatches and back again, loosening the L-shaped clamps. The bow thruster groaned as the ship slowly maneuvered into position for docking. The cold rain and icy wind pelted us viciously and made us wish we were back in our bunks. Against a black sky, the yellow deck lights outlined the ship's silhouette. The bosun climbed up on the hatch crane

Ojibway offloading supplies to the *Leon Fraser* just below the Soo Locks. (Courtesy of the photographer, Fred Hill)

(the "iron deckhand") to remove the hatch covers. This machine straddled the width of the deck and rolled on steel rails. Lining the crane up with each hatch, the bosun lifted the steel covers and set them down between the coamings.

Meanwhile, Red had coiled all the heaving lines to make ready for docking. The large steel cables had been wound off the winches and run through the chocks. The rope for the bosun's chair was strung through a long boom and tied off on a cleat. As we neared the docking area, the first mate, John McDonough, paced the deck, checking the reception on his walkie-talkie. He was a cherub-faced, jolly sort of fellow who liked a good laugh. In his white coveralls and white hardhat, he had an air of authority. It was three in the morning, and the ship had suddenly come to life.

As the bow of the ship approached the dock, I joined the other two deckhands as they hopped up on the first hatch, waiting to be swung over the side of the ship on the bosun's chair. A long, inch-and-a-half-thick line was strung through the eyes of a twenty-foot boom and tied to a wooden seat that looked like a piece of two-by-eight lumber. As we edged within five feet of the dock, the bosun gave the signal, one of the deckhands jumped up on the chair, and the boom swung out over the ship's side. When it was my turn, I was told to hang on tightly and look straight ahead. It was a twenty-five-foot drop to the water. As my feet were about to touch the dock, I felt a dockworker grab hold of my life jacket to help ease me down. Climbing off the chair, I slipped suddenly on the marblelike taconite pellets that were scattered around and toppled to the ground. "Here! Catch this," a watchman yelled from up on deck as he hurled a coiled heaving line towards me. In the dim, murky light, I could barely make out the form as it curled towards me. The docks appeared to be lighted by a few twenty-five-watt bulbs that flickered high overhead. From the pilothouse, the captain goosed the bow thruster to hold the nose of the ship against the dock. Once we had hold of the steel cables, the other two deckhands and I dragged them up the dock about twenty feet and looped them over the bollards. The mates buzzed back and forth on their walkie-talkies, trying to position the boat for unloading. "Twenty-four . . . Twelve . . . Six feet . . . Hang on!" With both hands straight overhead as if he were signaling a touchdown, the first mate called for the ship to stop right there. The four steam winches hissed and ratcheted loudly as they locked their positions and tugged the ship into place. After securing the head wire from the bow and the stern line back aft, we clambered back aboard to clean up and head to our bunks for a little shut-eye. We felt weary and grumpy, and we knew the watch would be calling us in a few short hours to close the hatches and hose down the deck.

For the next six or seven hours, four gigantic grasshopper-like Hulett unloaders reached deep into the cargo holds and feasted on 18,000 tons of taconite pellets from the Mesabi Range of northern Minnesota. They finished it off by lowering several caterpillar tractors into the hold to scrape and plow the stray pellets from the unreachable corners. They made so much noise all night that I couldn't sleep even with two pillows over my head. Moaning and groaning and banging and scraping the steel bulkheads, the machines worked with a vengeance. There was no escape. So I rolled out of my warm bed and wandered down to the galley for coffee and some early-morning scuttlebutt.

By noon, the *Leon Fraser* was underway, headed back to Duluth for another load. As we cleared the

Hulett iron ore unloaders at the Pennsylvania Railroad ore docks, Cleveland, Ohio, May 1943. (Photo part of the Farm Security Administration – Office of War Information Collection at the Library of Congress.) (Source: downloaded from http://wn.wikipedia.org/wiki/Image:Huletts.jpg)

breakwall at the entrance to the harbor, the wind began to pick up. Dirty Dan was operating the iron deckhand, and I was helping to pin the hatch covers that he lowered into place. The trick to pinning the hatches was to position the steel alignment bar in opposite corners of the hatch cover; working together, the other deckhand and I tried to line the bar up quickly with the matching hole in the hatch coaming. Things were going fine for a short while, but soon the bosun was dropping the covers down so abruptly that our bars were getting jammed. I signaled for him to lift the hatch cover and relower it. Again the bar got stuck. The bosun jerked the cover back up in the air.

Leon Fraser, leaving the MacArthur Lock in the Soo, 1981.
(Courtesy of the photographer, Fred Hill)

I knew he was getting really steamed now. Finally, on the third attempt, we had it maneuvered almost to the right position, but it was still slightly tilted and wouldn't drop down. From the far side of the deck, the bosun grabbed a nearby monkey wrench and hurled it wildly over my head into the lake. He leaped out of his seat on the hatch crane. "Jump on it, you sonofabitch!" he screamed. "Jump on it!" I wasn't quite sure how I, a hundred-and-forty-one-pound virtual featherweight, was going to budge this giant slab of steel by jumping on it. But, *why not*, I thought. *I'll give it a try.* I bounded up on the hatch like King Kong and began to jump up and down. It did not move even a quarter inch. The bosun glared across the deck at me with his jaw hanging open.

"Not you, you goddam mosquito! Red! Red! Where the hell is Red?" I went quietly back to my spot and awaited the stocky deckwatch. At two hundred and eighty pounds, Red appeared on deck within minutes, took one step on the hatch cover, and snapped it into place. He glanced around smugly and disappeared without a word.

Finding My Bearings

It took me the better part of a month to start feeling the least bit comfortable working as a deckhand aboard the *Leon Fraser*. Without knowing the language, it was like living in a foreign country. Art, my roommate, served as my interpreter while I tried to learn the nautical jargon in this strange new land.

Early on I discovered that there was a definite pecking order on board. The deck, engine, and galley departments each had their own hierarchy. The captain and the mates were the officers of the deck department, which was rounded out by the wheelsmen, watchmen, deckwatches, bosun, and deckhands. Together, they were responsible for navigating, loading, unloading, and general maintenance on the ship. Their quarters were located on the forward end. Their counterpart, the engine department, included the engineers, oilers, and wipers, and they lived on the after end. The chief engineer served as the head honcho, and he made sure that the monstrous ship's engine ran smoothly and was maintained meticulously.

The overall morale of the crew was in the hands of the galley department. The chief cook, second cook, and porters could make the difference between a good-spirited, contented crew and a surly bunch of whiners and complainers. Working three separate shifts every day, these guys cooked and served breakfast, lunch, and dinner around the clock. On many mornings out on the lakes, the second cook would whip up a few batches of oatmeal-raisin cookies, cinnamon rolls, and apple pies. These heady aromas were wonderfully intoxicating within fifty feet of the galley. Every Saturday night, T-bone steaks or porterhouses were served with baked potatoes and trimmings. Crew members could always have as much as they wanted. No dietician was standing by to question the calories or the cholesterol. And we loaded up. So it came as no surprise to learn that putting on extra weight was clearly an occupational hazard. Regardless, there was never a complaint from the crew.

With the exception of deckhands, all deck and engine crew members stood watches of four hours on and eight hours off, changing watches at 12:00, 4:00, and 8:00. The ship's bell above the pilothouse always rang eight bells at the change of watch. The count then started over again, that is, one bell at the half-hour, two bells at the full hour, and so on until the next watch changed at eight bells. Deckhands could be called out at any hour, depending on what time we came into port or locked through the Soo. Otherwise, we worked our eight-hour shift out on the open lakes. I really didn't mind waking up at odd hours to work; the change of pace made for a more interesting day. However, because of these unusual hours, our circadian rhythms never had a chance to catch up.

I quickly learned my port from my starboard, fore and aft, above and below decks. Before long, I was able to tie various knots, such as a slip knot on a heaving line, a bowline, a pair of half hitches, and a clove hitch. Much trickier was learning the art of splicing an eye on the end of a rope or lashing a nylon whipping on the end of a frayed line. But with a little practice, I finally got the hang of those, too.

One week, when a deckwatch had to get off the boat for a family emergency, I was asked to fill in for him. At 4:00 in the morning, I started my cleaning stations by sweeping and mopping up the dunnage room and the hallways. It was a cool starry night with the wind picking up considerably. It was so quiet I felt like I had the entire boat to myself and could work at my own pace. I walked back aft, dumped the trash on the fantail, and made a batch of coffee in the galley. I leaned into the wind with my head down as I made my way back up the deck. One of my duties as deck-watch was to clean out the large brass spittoon in the pilothouse. For several hours on watch, the first mate and wheelsman had been chewing their share of Red

Man and spitting the residue into the brass receptacle. I entered the wheelhouse, said good morning, and grabbed the half-full spittoon with both hands. As I carried it carefully down the two sets of stairs to the main deck, I tried to keep from spilling any of the slimy contents on my clothes. With a brisk motion, I hurled the sloppy, disgusting spew over the side just in time for a gust of wind to catch it and hurl it back in my face. I stood there dripping for a moment and glanced around to see if anyone had witnessed this sad event. After that humbling little episode, I always remembered to walk on the leeward side of the ship, away from the prevailing wind. Also, I learned early to never put my hands in my pockets when strolling down the deck. The stanchions, or short fences along the main deck, offer little protection against falling over the side of the ship if someone stumbles on one of the raised deck plates. It has happened more than once. Anyone falling into Lake Superior in late November wouldn't stand much of a chance. A life jacket might only prolong the agony.

In the mid-1970s, on a downbound lake freighter, a deckwatch from the Soo apparently tripped on deck during the night and fell over the wire railing into Lake Superior. It was midsummer and the water was still frigid. Fortunately, when this accident occurred, the man's ship was rounding Keewenaw Point, a long arm of land that juts out into Lake Superior. The freighter passed within five miles of Copper

Harbor at the tip of the peninsula. This all happened so quickly, with no witnesses, that several hours had passed before anyone on board was aware that the deckwatch was missing. Bobbing in the frigid lake water, he saw his ship sailing away from him into the night. Realizing that there was no chance of alerting anyone, the deckwatch turned his attention to the light beam flashing from Copper Harbor five miles away. Hypothermia might have set in quickly in the chilly night waters had he not been such a strong swimmer. Guided by the flashing light, he managed to swim all the way to shore and survive the ordeal. For years, there were rumors that, as a stunt, he had intentionally jumped off the ship with scuba gear. Some thought it was just too convenient that he "fell off" near Keewenaw Point. However, the truth, as I learned from his father years later, was that it was simply an embarrassing accident that he was incredibly lucky to survive. He had merely stumbled over a raised deck plate and catapulted over the railing. Nothing preplanned—just a close call.

⚓ ⚓ ⚓

One tough thing about being a greenhorn was not only did I have to bumble my way through all the new nautical slang, but I also had to prove myself over a thirty-day probationary period before I would be allowed to join the union. Union membership in Local 5000 of the United Steelworkers of America was required for employment on the boats. So that's why the bosun was always challenging me, to see how much frustration I could take. He wanted to get under my skin enough so I would quit and go back home. It was a game of survival for him, and he was out to break my will if he could. As it turned out, the bosun didn't like any guys from the Soo who came on board. He'd seen too many college students who came out for a few months to make a quick buck and then disappeared. Or slackers who worked only long enough to pay for the parties and a new set of wheels back home. He resented them all, and he let them know it. Dirty Dan had worked on the boats for sixteen years and had earned the right to become boatswain of the deck crew. He was proud of that; yet, I think he felt tied down by the demands of the long shipping season from April through December. These short-timers could come and go as they pleased. No commitments. Dan supported a family back in Minnesota. Sometimes, it may not have seemed quite fair to him, and he envied the short-timers. He swore a blue streak at them every chance he got. And I gave him plenty of chances—like the time he walked up to me one morning as I was painting on deck and asked, "Where's Red?" I pointed up towards the forward end, hesitated, and said, "I think he's down in the basement." He glared at me, scratched his balls, and said, "What the fuck? Down in the what? You asshole rookies! Always the same old shit!" And he stomped away muttering to himself. As Crazy Dog often said, "We're all here because we're not all there." Sometimes it seemed that the harder I tried to fit in, the more trouble I made for myself.

Lifelines and Buoys

Lifeline: *noun* 1) a rope or line thrown in to rescue someone in difficulties in water or used by sailors to secure themselves to a boat. 2) a thing which is essential for the continued existence of someone or something or which provides a means of escape.

⚓ ⚓ ⚓

It wasn't always easy being cooped up with thirty-some other guys, living and working on a Great Lakes ore boat for months at a time. Some of us would get a little stir-crazy. And woman crazy. All we could think about sometimes were the good times we'd have once we got our feet back on solid ground. Daydreaming and fantasizing soon became favorite obsessions. Anything to escape the long stretches of time that hung before us as we sailed from port to port, loading, unloading, and loading once again. It's as if we were in a state of suspended animation, waiting patiently for the spell to be broken so we could resume our normal lives.

From time to time, a letter from home would arrive, bringing news about who got married, who was arrested for drunk driving, or who just came back to town. A little news like that seemed to go a long way towards fighting off some of the loneliness and the sense of isolation. Some of the guys in the deck crew would simply lie on their bunks after dinner, have a smoke, and cross off another day on their calendars with a black magic marker. When I saw this, I wondered if they also wanted bars installed in place of the doorways and portholes. During the hustle and bustle of the workday out on deck, the boredom and the sense of isolation never seemed to occur. However, once the day's work was finished, the hours could seem endless. We played a lot of cribbage, usually for a nickel a point. Some of the guys just drank a few Pabst Blue Ribbons and traded odd stories and gossip for hours on end. After awhile, I became good friends with some of the crew and began to develop a sense of family with all my shipmates. I worked with them night and day, ate and slept with them, and raised holy hell with these guys uptown in the bars. Though mostly unspoken and unacknowledged, there was a feeling of connection and camaraderie that settled in.

⚓ ⚓ ⚓

Every family lives through its share of hard times. Whenever I am facing a difficult time or a daunting task, I try to remember that I have been blessed with a healthy dose of Finnish *sisu.* I was born in the Upper Peninsula of Michigan, home of one of the largest Finnish-American populations in the country. Being from the U.P., we are fondly known as Yoopers. Those folks from the Lower Peninsula, below the Mackinac Bridge, are called trolls. In the mid-nineteenth century, iron ore was discovered near Negaunee, a small town in the central Upper Peninsula. As a result, a great number of Finns, Germans, and Swedes moved to that area for jobs in the mining industry. Due to the many bleak winters in their native Finland, the various wars fought with Russia, and the overall inhospitable climate, the Finns developed strength of will and perseverance that is known today as *sisu.* Some say it means determination or decisiveness to get things done against impossible odds. Others say it's just pigheaded stubbornness. But I feel that sisu gives me a special strength and will to get through hard times without complaining.

Perhaps my sisu was inherited, or maybe it was honed through my experiences growing up in Sault Ste. Marie. With three brothers and a sister, I was the youngest of the brood, which was looked after mainly by my mother. My father served in the Army and was stationed halfway across the country. We didn't get to see him very often. Our family lived very modestly, the kids passing down their clothes and boots to the next youngest one to save a few dollars. We seemed to move to a new place every couple of years, always renting a cheap house somewhere on the south side of town. We didn't own a car, we mostly walked everywhere— to school, downtown, to friends' houses. We did have a car back in 1957 for a short while, an Oldsmobile, but that didn't last long after Dad drove it home one night after a few too many drinks. Mom put it up for sale the next day. I guess she figured our legs were more reliable and quite a bit safer.

To save money one Christmas, we didn't buy a tree. Then on Christmas Eve, after all the tree lots in town were closed for the night, my three brothers and I walked through the snowy streets down to the Tastee Freeze. There was a cardboard sign on a post that said "Free." We picked out the best looking Charlie Brown Scotch pine we could find and dragged it home, singing Christmas carols and throwing snowballs most of the way. Once it was decorated and strung with colored lights, it was one of the prettiest trees ever. It was a great Christmas. We all received new hockey sticks, chukes, and choppers from Santa. Under a dim streetlight, we played boot hockey with all the neighborhood kids until Mom called us in for Christmas dinner.

Not one to complain easily, Mom certainly had her own share of sisu. Of course, she thought of it as her Irish stubbornness. Quite often I watched her trudging up the street with a sack of groceries in each hand, walking the five blocks from the A&P to our little house on Tweed Street. She washed clothes in our four-legged Speed Queen wringer-washer and hung them to dry in the backyard. She shopped and made meals for all five of us, and attended all of the parent-teacher conferences regularly. During our junior high and high school years, Mom usually packed sack lunches for each of us consisting of two sandwiches and an apple or Twinkie. The sandwiches were mainly the peanut butter and jelly or bologna and cheese variety. Over the years, at that rate, we calculated that she packed over eight thousand sandwiches for us. And when that part of the day was over, Mom caught a cab and went to work part-time as a waitress at the Flair Restaurant or as a hatcheck girl down at the Northview Lounge. She must have been exhausted. But she rarely complained and then only about needing a little more money to make ends meet. She was the lifeblood, the driving force, behind our family. There was nothing she wouldn't do for her kids.

At times, it was necessary for us to stretch a dollar to get by for a while and then to stretch it a little further. We didn't always have a choice. When I was six years old, my family moved back to the Soo from Wurzburg, Germany, where my father had been stationed for two years. We rented a three-room apartment for the six of us; my mother told the landlord there were only three of us altogether. In the living room was a Murphy bed that dropped down from behind the closet doors. My three brothers and I slept in that spring-loaded nest like bedbugs, fighting for territory and covers all night long. Since it was early October and the apple trees were bursting, we hiked up to Eagle's Woods and filled several duffel bags. Over the next few weeks, Mom magically transformed our harvest into baked apples, apple pies, and applesauce. We never got tired of a good thing. To help out with the food budget, my sister's boyfriend shot a partridge for dinner but forgot to remove all the buckshot. Between sorting out all the pellets on our plates and trying partridge for the first time, it turned out to be a rather exotic meal.

Although there were some extreme circumstances from time to time, we usually saw the humor in them. As long as we could get a good story and a laugh out of it, we could cope with almost anything. Mom had a knack for staying one step ahead of the landlord when he came around to collect the rent. Since her government check from Dad never arrived until the first week of the month, money was very tight at that time. Some of the bills simply had to be postponed. On many winter mornings, we woke up to freezing rooms. We had run out of fuel oil and had to wait for the fuel man to come. The air was so frigid one morning that my pet turtle from Woolworth's, kept in a small dish with a little plastic palm tree, had frozen solid. He had retreated from the cold water into his tiny shell, only to become suspended in an icy prison on our coffee table. Mom told us to get to school quickly, where it was warm. Meanwhile, she scrambled back into bed under a stack of woolen blankets and coats to await the fuel man.

When school let out for the year, I always looked forward to a long summer of reading comics, eating ice cream, and building forts with my friends. One of the highlights of every summer was the annual trip out to Sherman Park. We woke up early to pack our picnic lunch of hot dogs, potato salad, baked beans, chips, and Kool-Aid. In addition to the customary swimming suits, masks, and snorkels, we made sure we brought our football, baseball bats, gloves, and balls, as well as towels and a radio. By the time John, the Yellow Cab driver, showed up, we had all the paraphernalia neatly piled next to the curb. Mom and the five of us crammed into the cab and headed proudly for Sherman Park. It was a journey of sheer will and logistics. All afternoon, we played baseball, then football, practiced the cannonball dive off "the rock," built sand castles on the beach, and played on the sprawling porch at the park's log pavilion. After swimming and picnicking at the park until almost dark, John arrived to haul us home. Mom tipped the cabdriver an extra fifty cents for going out of his way.

Through the years, the Finnish traits I've inherited have helped me overcome difficult odds. A certain perseverance took shape in me that has favored me in both school and sports. Schoolwork never came easy, but I always felt that if I pushed myself hard I could achieve better results. Longer hours studying and persistence eventually paid off with improved grades. Even the notorious Finnish shyness has played a role; it made me work harder in other areas, such as schoolwork, to make up for a social awkwardness with girls. It's like the old joke: "How do you recognize a Finnish extrovert? He looks at *your* shoes." I may have missed a few things looking down, but it helps a Finn to concentrate. Each of us moves at a different pace. We go with our strengths and play down our weaknesses. Running cross-country in high school, for example, I was no Paavo Nurmi, but I felt the same determination nevertheless and always drove myself to the finish line.

During my family's early years, Dad was stationed in the army. From Washington, D.C., or Fort Sill, Oklahoma, he wrote letters to us from time to time. My parents didn't get along quite so well as I would have liked; so maybe, in a way, the distance between them was a blessing. At best, they tolerated each other. How I wound up with four siblings has always been a mystery to me. I used to wonder if I was the product of immaculate conception. But then, the stork sounded more plausible. Dad sometimes visited for a week at Christmas time, riding for several days on the bucking backseat of a Greyhound bus. Between the smoky swirl of cigars and a six-pack of Stroh's beer, my father braved the icy streets to play a game of winter football with us. Wearing a T-shirt and a pair of leather slippers, he was no match for the will of four rambunctious boys, who tackled him headlong into the snowbank. Some mornings, he treated us to pop and chips down at Hallesy's Bar while he tuned up with an early hair of the dog. But too soon, he boarded the bus and vanished for another year. "OK, troops," he'd say, "You hold the fort and take care of the ol' Ma." My father seemed more like a distant uncle to me and my brothers and sister, never wanting to get too close to any of us. As we got older, we knew we were missing something but weren't really sure what it was. I missed him a lot every year and thought, perhaps, he felt lonely as well. One of the greatest things I envied about my dad was his keen sense of humor. Rarely did he miss the opportunity to make a quip or pull a practical joke. His dry wit is one thing I may have gratefully inherited from him.

Through my father, I have a direct connection to the iron ore industry that goes back two generations. On the morning of November 3, 1926, the worst mining disaster in Michigan history took place at the Barnes-Hecker mine near Ishpeming in the central Upper Peninsula. When the underground shaft filled with water and collapsed, one man survived the cave-in; of the fifty-one who died, only ten of their bodies were ever recovered. My grandfather, William Hill, was the mine inspector for Marquette County and

Headline in *The Daily Mining Journal*, November 4, 1926;
the day after the Barnes-Hecker mine disaster. (Source:
The Mining Journal; Marquette, MI)

was making safety checks at the time of the tragedy.
My father was only twelve years old in 1926, and his
father meant a lot to him. At lunchtime, he had often
looked forward to racing down to the mine to deliver
his father a hot pasty wrapped in a linen cloth. This
terrible accident and loss of their father and husband
shattered him, his two brothers, his sister, and his
mother. Altogether 132 children were left fatherless;
42 women were widowed.

Today a stone memorial honoring all those miners
who died in the tragedy stands near the Michigan
Mine Industry Museum in Negaunee. In some ways,
my father never fully recovered from that event. It

haunted him as he tried to build a relationship with his own family. One evening, when I was in my twenties, my father sat quietly in the living room nursing a glass of wine. Lost in some kind of reverie, he said to me, "Never get too close to anyone; you might lose them someday." I hadn't realized how deeply these events had affected him, and that he was still feeling a painful loss after all those years. His Finnish sisu and stoicism had helped him survive the hard times.

In a similar way, my siblings and I couldn't help but develop a sense of survival and an ability to adapt to less-than-perfect circumstances. To this day, I feel that if I suddenly lost everything I owned, all of my material possessions, I would adjust to it and come out doing just fine. That loss alone could not change my spirit or the way I see life. Growing up, my family never got used to a high standard of living. We lived modestly, not desperately, but always proudly. We never felt any shame despite our humble circumstances. On the contrary, we always enjoyed the humor and great stories that emerged from awkward family situations. After all, we are Yoopers, with sisu to boot.

Red Lead and Sougee

For the most part, Great Lakes ore carriers are very well maintained, both inside and out. True boat watchers around the lakes have always noticed that by midsummer most ships have been dressed in a fresh coat of red lead paint. The white-painted cabins on the bow and stern always appear well scrubbed. By contrast, most of the saltwater ships that pass through the Soo Locks look bruised and beaten, rusting away from years of neglect. An observer might wonder if the deckhands have ever lifted a chipper or a paintbrush.

From fit-out to layup, the painting never seemed to end on an ore boat. If the weather allowed, the deck crew was usually chipping and painting somewhere on deck. On a sunny day in July on Lake Superior, with the wind blowing steadily, it could feel like thirty-five degrees windchill. We had to dress in several layers of sweatshirts, coats, chukes, and gloves to stay warm until coffee time. Some mornings we lay on our backs to chip the flaking undersides of the hatch covers. If they were in pretty rough shape, we were spitting paint chips all day. We took advantage of any warm afternoon to roll the decks and hatch covers with heavy-duty red lead paint. It was an oil-based paint with nonskid sand added to it for traction. Before long, most of my work clothes had a healthy splattering of red lead. But I was proud of it. Kind of like a football player with turf stuck to his helmet and mud on his uniform. It was proof I had played the game.

One afternoon, as we were painting the winches on the forward end, I reached way underneath to paint a difficult area. One of the deckhands looked at me, grabbed my bucket, and hurled the paint beneath the greasy winch. He swished it around quickly, threw the brush in the empty bucket, and yelled, "Fuck that shit! It's coffee time. What are you, some kind of company man? This is good enough for a fucking steamboat." Well, there's no arguing with that logic. So we headed back to the galley for java.

Upon leaving port after loading or unloading our cargo, the deck crew was responsible for cleaning up the taconite pellets that were strewn all over the deck. One good slip on those little marbles and a guy could crack his melon open. We all climbed into our Sorel boots and yellow rain gear and stretched the hot-water hoses out on the deck. Crazy Dog, the watchman, led the charge. Over six hundred feet of deck had to be hosed off clean, about a two-or-three-hour job. With two deckhands pulling hose behind him, Crazy Dog went to work with gusto, aiming the powerful fire hose and spraying the black grimy sludge and pellets off the hatches, down the deck, and out the scupper holes. He really loved this job. He tried to shoot for distance, aiming the hose in a long watery arc at a few stray marbles five hatches away, that is, until the bosun spied him and told him to get his ass in gear.

After hosing down, it was time to fill up our sougee buckets and scrub the white work on the captain's deck as well as the pilothouse. Sougee was a type of powdery soap that was so harsh it created a red itchy rash on contact. The deck crew hated it. But we couldn't escape it. It trickled down our coat sleeves and splashed on our faces. We could even taste it. But sougee kept the white work bright and shiny and made the old man happy. So who were we to complain?

One nice thing about decking was the wide variety of work. One day we're greasing the wheel chains that connect the steering in the pilothouse to the rudder; another day, we're painting the smokestack or the draft numbers on the bow. Occasionally, we found ourselves oiling hundreds of rusty hatch clamps to keep them working smoothly or stenciling numbers or letters on the bulkheads for safety. Never a shortage of work to do. On the other hand, we had to make sure the bosun never caught us loafing or "fucking the dog," as he called it. We'd see him hulking down the deck, hunched over slightly in his flannel shirt and blue jeans, long muscular arms swinging at his side like a Neanderthal. He'd scratch his butt cheeks and spit over the rail. Dirty Dan had a reputation for being pretty rough on new deckhands. A new recruit had thirty days to prove himself in Dan's eyes before he could join the union. Until then he was on his own. The bosun had told more than a few lazy deckhands, "Pack your bags, numb-nuts. I'm puttin' your ass off at the Soo!" He had the power to fire people on the spot. The best idea was to stay out of his way. After a guy had worked his thirty days and received his union card, he could address any grievance he had with his ship's union representative. In our case, the union rep was the bosun himself. Case closed.

There were a number of times that the bosun confronted one of the deckhands for not doing something exactly as he had ordered. On more than a few occasions, Dirty Dan had grabbed the paint bucket and brush out of someone's hands and flung them wildly into the lake. Hammers, wrenches, scrapers—everything was fair game to him when he was angry with one of us. It was some kind of great temperamental release for him to pitch things over the side. Who knows how much U.S. Steel lost in tools and materials over the years due to this guy's erratic behavior? Most of us learned to stay clear of him. But Gary, one of the other deckhands, was not one to back down from anybody. During one trip, as we were departing Duluth around midnight, Gary and I were busy tying off the boarding ladder up on the boat deck. We were having a little trouble lowering the ladder with the winch when the bosun suddenly appeared out of nowhere. He shoved Gary out of his way and tried to take over. Gary turned on Dan, picked him up by the lapels of his coat, slammed him against the bulkhead and shrieked, "Listen, you sonofabitch! Don't you ever touch me again! You do, motherfucker, and I'll throw you over the side so fast you won't know what hit you!" The bosun, stunned, backed off and stumbled away speechless. Few of the guys had ever confronted the bosun eyeball to eyeball. Dan didn't know what to make of it. Never again did he bother Gary, who kept his guard up even more now. He was like a wounded animal that's been cornered, ready to lash out at any perceived threat.

Off Course and Drifting

When learning anything new, it takes awhile to work out all the kinks. Luckily, I had the advantage of being eighteen years old and thought I had learned most shipboard duties faster than the average bear. I strode down the deck with confidence and assurance, knowing my seaman's skills were growing by leaps and bounds. They say that a little bit of knowledge can be dangerous. How little I really knew.

One gray misty morning, the *Leon Fraser* was approaching the breakwall in Duluth. Tourists and locals gathered near the pier to wave and enthusiastically welcome any returning ship. As if we'd been gone for many months instead of just a week, they hollered their hellos to the crew. It was great to be welcomed back. The trip from the breakwall to the loading dock took about thirty minutes, cruising under the aerial bridge and through the twisting ship canal.

After the deckhands were swung over the side on the bosun's chair, we landed on the dock and tied her up. The loading chutes dropped down immediately, emptying the loaded train cars suspended on the trestle high overhead. In a roaring cloud of dust, the taconite cargo rumbled into the ship's hold. The first mate kept two of the deckhands down on the dock to pull cables when we shifted the boat. The ore had to be loaded evenly into the ship's holds so she didn't get a "belly" or a "hog," too much weight in the center or on either end. The boat was shifted twenty or thirty feet back and forth on the pier to line up with various loading chutes. I stood by down on the dock, waiting to pull cable when the order came. Despite my hard-soled work boots, walking safely on the taconite-strewn dock was a real gamble. Pellets occasionally fell from the trestle above, bouncing off my hardhat. Once I placed the eye of the cable over the bollard, I moved away quickly as the watchman tightened up the wires with the powerful winches. I had been warned that if a steel cable ever snapped, it could rip my head off instantly if I happened to be standing in the wrong place.

It was sometimes half an hour between shifts. To kill time down on the dock, I often memorized poems or wrote letters in my head. Reading some of the graffiti scrawled on the dock timbers by other deckhands was always an entertaining way to pass the time. One message read, "God is not dead. He thinks he's captain on the *A. H. Ferbert*." Or another offering: "For a good time, call Lulu at 549-6836. For a

Approaching the Duluth breakwall, 1986.
(From personal collection)

better time, call Hank at 549-6629." Finally, the mate
called us back on board while the engineers pumped
out the ballast tanks. He told us to go have coffee for
twenty minutes if we liked. Since I'd already drunk
several cups earlier, I decided to head up to my room
to talk to Art, the deckwatch, for a few minutes. He
was lying in his bunk reading when I walked in and
sat down. While we talked, I kept my life jacket and
hardhat on. Within minutes, the door to our cabin
flew open, and there stood Dirty Dan glaring at me
with this wild-eyed maniacal look. He bounded into
the room in two swift steps, grabbed me by my life
jacket with both fists, and yanked me through the
doorway. My feet left the deck. He heaved me up the

dunnage stairway like a load of dirty laundry. "You rotten sonofabitch! You don't go back to bed when you're on break!" he bellowed, "The mate's looking for you on deck. Jesus Christ, I don't fuckin' believe it." I mumbled some pathetic defense, but I was so rattled I wasn't making complete sense. By the time this story made the rounds, the bosun was telling everyone that I had actually crawled back in bed and gone to sleep. Thank God my thirty days probation was nearly up.

Over the next week or so, I tried not to make any glaring mistakes. I felt like I was walking on hot coals, and the only remedy was to grow thicker skin. All of us stayed out of the bosun's way as much as possible, but we couldn't avoid him entirely. He was the boss of the deck crew. Whenever he ran into one of us in port at one of the bars, Dirty Dan was our best friend, all buddy-buddy. He would buy drinks, slap us on the back, and even play a game of pool. But once we were back on the ship, and he was roaring drunk, he turned from Dr. Jeckyl to Mr. Hyde. We couldn't move fast enough; we couldn't jump high enough; we simply couldn't please him. So, we basically did our jobs and tried to steer clear of his path.

Sometimes we loaded in Two Harbors, Minnesota, where an old tugboat named the *Edna G.* cruised out to nudge us safely into the harbor. When she blew her whistle, she sounded a rich bass tone that rattled the wooden dock timbers and echoed across the harbor

Duluth ore docks. (From personal collection)

like Barry White. It was a deep, almost mournful, whistle that wheezed out of her lungs, so eerie it gave me chills. The *Edna G.* belonged in a Humphrey Bogart movie with shrouds of fog and shadows and shady characters down on the waterfront. In Duluth, the *Fraser* was able to maneuver with her bow thruster well enough that she didn't require a tugboat.

As soon as we had tied up to the dock, the bumboat pulled alongside and was open for business. The two Kaner brothers were a couple of ambitious entrepreneurs who had put together a business that catered to the needs of the sailors. If a crew member were off watch or on break, he could scramble down the short ladder that was hooked on the ship's gunnels and onto the bumboat. There was nothing fancy or polished on the Kaners' boat, just a few basic necessities and some highly desirable luxuries. Of course, razor blades, shaving cream, and other toiletries could be found. And then there was the extensive library of reading material, magazines like *Penthouse, Gallery, Beaver, Sex To Sixty* and paperbacks like *The Tender Flesh*. Most crew members popped a beer and exchanged boating stories with the Kaners, catching up on the news about other U.S. Steel ships that had docked there recently.

Before heading back up the ladder to work, we'd order two cases of Pabst Blue Ribbon to be sent up to the deckhands' room. This was done right in front of the mates; no one seemed to mind as long as we were discreet and did our work properly. Attached to one of the bulkheads on the main deck up forward was a sign that read "No Alcohol Allowed On Board Ship." Although just about everyone on the boat drank a few beers or shots of whiskey regularly, no one did it out in the open. If alcohol were truly banned, it would be very difficult to keep a crew aboard all season long.

For a slight change of pace, we'd pick up a few bottles of cheap red wine. After work one evening, as we steamed quietly across the dark lake, I tied a bottle of wine in a long wet sock with a heaving line. Opening the porthole in our room, I slowly lowered the bottle into the waves splashing off the bow. In about five minutes, I hauled it back up, ready to uncork this fine vintage. The wet sock was icy cold from

The tug *Edna G.* at the ore docks in Two Harbors, Minnesota; September, 1957. (Courtesy of the photographer, Al Anderson)

the lake water, but all that remained was a sockful of broken green glass. After that waste of good wine, we stuck to aluminum beer cans in a mesh net. It was amazing that you could cool a beer down from room temperature to almost freezing within two minutes.

I learned not to get too cocky with what few sailing skills I had acquired. There was more to know than I had ever dreamed. Though I had humiliated myself on more than one occasion, I knew that the bosun and I would probably tangle horns again. Dirty Dan never hesitated cussing a guy out or putting him in his place. If Dan was agitated, he would just as soon throw someone over the side or heave a crescent wrench at him. I was able to handle it only one day at a time without going a little loony.

Going Up The Street

What Shall We Do With A Drunken Sailor?
(traditional sea shanty)

What shall we do with the drunken sailor?
What shall we do with the drunken sailor?
What shall we do with the drunken sailor?
Earl-eye in the morning?

Way hay and up she rises
Way hay and up she rises
Way hay and up she rises
Earl-eye in the morning!

Throw him in the brig until he's sober
Throw him in the brig until he's sober
Throw him in the brig until he's sober
Earl-eye in the morning!

Shave his balls with a rusty razor
Shave his balls with a rusty razor
Shave his balls with a rusty razor
Earl-eye in the morning!

Put him in bed with the Captain's daughter
Put him in bed with the Captain's daughter
Put him in bed with the Captain's daughter
Earl-eye in the morning!

Sooner or later, for your own sanity, you have to get away. Living and working twenty-four hours a day with thirty other guys takes its toll. You can't jump in your car and head downtown for a movie. You can't call up a few friends and meet at the restaurant for dinner. You can't take your girlfriend out for dancing and a few drinks. No, the ship is pretty much your entire world. It's not only your workplace, it's your home, your social network, your entertainment, and your gymnasium, all depending on how you want to use it. When you finally get into port and you have a few hours of free time, you have to get away from the boat and go up the street to see what you can find.

A full trip—loading, unloading, and back again—takes about five or six days to complete. From Duluth or Two Harbors on the western tip of Lake Superior, we traveled eastward to the Soo, down the St. Mary's

U.S. Steel steamboat (hatch farm) pivoting in the turning basin; Gary, Indiana. (Photo by Fred G. Korth, Courtesy of U.S. Steel Corp)

River, and through Lake Michigan to usually Gary or South Chicago. Alternately, we made hauls down Lake Huron, through the St. Clair and Detroit Rivers, and across Lake Erie to usually Conneaut or Lorain.

When we pulled into port, most guys headed for the nearest bar to have a few drinks, play some pool, listen to a few songs on the jukebox, and make a phone call to their girlfriends or wives. We usually had about five or six hours while we were unloading the cargo, long enough to get into trouble one way or another. One typical night in Conneaut, a couple deckhands and I strolled up the street to Shaky Eddy's Bar, a block or so from the docks. Shaky Eddy was there, hustling up and down delivering drinks to the crew along the bar. He was a short guy with horn-rimmed glasses, half balding, with a thin shock of gray hair. His movements were quick and jerky, and his eyes darted around the room like a squirrel guarding its nuts. Clearly, he was happy, if not a little bit nervous, about the sudden rush of business. We ordered a round of beers and plunked a few quarters in the jukebox. Ike and Tina belted out "Proud Mary," and before long, couples were up dancing around the tables. Soon the mates and the bosun showed up, along with a watchman and a few engineers. The drinks were flying around freely, each man trying to outdo the next by buying another round. It seemed like over half the crew was here now, reveling in this party atmosphere. Cigar smoke swirled around the room like toxic ether, obscuring the neon lights behind the bar. The waitress happily collected her ten-and twenty-dollar tips from the high-spirited but pickled boaters. The money was meant to be spent, not hoarded. And Shaky Eddy grinned every time the cash register rang.

At some point, being cooped up on the boats makes everybody very horny, just itching to go up the street at the next port and find some action. In Lorain one night, a bunch of the guys called a taxi down to the docks and headed for a place called "The Tropicana" in the red-light part of town. It was referred to as getting your ashes hauled, your carrot chewed, or putting lead in your pencil. We met them back at the "Angry Bull" for a few beers, and everyone was smiling from ear to ear. So I guess they enjoyed themselves. With a faraway look and a glint in his eye, one of the watchmen boasted, "When I kick the bucket, I want to die making love to a beautiful redhead, with my hands wrapped around a pair of forty-four double-D's." Some things are worth dying for.

As soon as we got to port, those going uptown would line up near the boarding ladder back aft. The men usually glanced at the ETD, or estimated time of departure, on the small chalkboard before climbing down the ladder. Once the ship was loaded, the cables were thrown off, and we'd get underway quickly, waiting for no one. ETD was only estimated. Jerry, the deckwatch, otherwise known as Whiskey Man, found this out the hard way. Late one evening in Duluth, we had finished loading, and the captain immediately tooted the ship's whistle one short blast to let go all the mooring cables. The ship very slowly started drifting away from the pier. Suddenly, near the far end of the dock, a taxi pulled up in a cloud of dust and out jumped a guy carrying a box on his shoulder. In the dim light, he stumbled his way over the slippery taconite marbles strewn on the path. He yelled up to us, "Hey! Hold the boat! Hold the boat! I'm coming!" We were about five feet off the dock by now, and the first mate saw Jerry waving up to us and yelling. Quickly, we grabbed the ten-foot hook ladder and hung it over the side. "Throw down the parcel bag," he said. He loaded his box into the bag, then leaped across the water to the ladder. For as drunk as he was, it was a very athletic jump, and he clung to the ladder in a stubborn stupor. As we helped him climb safely aboard, the mate retrieved the box from the parcel bag. Jerry's half-shut eyes were bloodshot as he staggered from side to side. The box was a full case of Johnny Walker whiskey. He retrieved it from the mate and, without a word, wove his way up to his cabin. The next day, he was fired, and they put him off at the Soo.

However, all was not lost. The deckwatch inspired the following:

"Whiskey Man"

Whiskey Man, Whiskey Man, where do you roam?
From the Great Lakes freighters
to the bars back home,
From the Kaners' bumboat and
the ore docks of Duluth,
To the steel mills of Gary and
a bottle of vermouth.

As a deckwatch, you've somehow managed to last,
But the old man and the bosun are closing in fast,
You've rambled and stumbled
your way down the deck,
Your life has become a major train wreck.

What you really need now is a three-day pass,
That first mate is always riding your ass
Just one more screwup you know will be risky . . .
Ah, hell with it! Pass me that bottle of whiskey.

Sometimes, a guy can let his guard down and miss what's coming at him. In Gary one fall afternoon, we had just tied up the boat. The bosun needed the deckhands for some work before we headed up the street. Having less time than usual, we stopped first at "Jack's Tap" for a couple cold ones and a game of pool, then made our way around the corner to "The Trotter's Inn." This was a working-class bar whose only redeeming feature was cheap beer. A few of the regulars sat on their stools near the end of the bar. The barmaid was a hefty woman in a moo-moo dress who looked to be about two hundred and fifty pounds. For all we knew, she could have played linebacker for the Chicago Bears. Another deckhand and I nursed our beers for a few minutes, just enjoying the time away from the boat. As we listened to the jukebox, the barmaid worked her way towards us, leaned over the bar, and with a sincere expression on her plump face, said to me, "Can I ask you a personal question?" Not wanting to turn down a polite request, I said, "Sure. What is it?" She drew closer to me. "Tell me, honey, do you like to eat pussy?" I was stunned, but the other deckhand nearly fell off his stool laughing.

The woman cackled with delight and scooted over to the jukebox to pop a quarter in. She lifted her dress up to show her whale-sized undies and shook her booty to the music. We finished our beers, and I quickly dragged my friend out of there. It wasn't an image I wanted to prolong.

About a month later, I wound up in the same bar with a deckhand named George. He was from Pittsburgh and liked his share of music, especially Frank Sinatra. We stopped at "The Trotters" because a six-piece black soul band was playing on Saturday night. When we walked in, the band had a good groove going with Marvin Gaye's "What's Going On?" We sat at the bar, downing one after another. George was trying to tell me about some girlfriend of his back in Pittsburgh, but all I could think about was the Motown sound coming from this band. They were great.

I had played drums in several rock bands back in high school, and this band was really whetting my appetite for picking up the sticks again. As soon as the band took a break, I walked over and asked one of the musicians if I could sit in with them. He took one look at me, one of the only two white guys in the bar that night, and said, "Man, I don't think so. Be cool." And he walked away. After awhile, with the help of a few beers, I got up my courage and decided that wasn't good enough for me. I wanted to play those drums. So I staggered over to the bandstand, sat down at the drums, and began to sound out the beat for "In-A-Gadda-Da-Vida," a drum solo I remembered from my last band. A black bar manager ran over to me and anxiously pleaded, "Man, you can't do that shit! These guys got a show to put on. Now come on out of there!" So I went back to the bar to think it over. George was entertained by it all and bought another round.

Now, an all-black bar on a Saturday night in Gary, Indiana, was not quite the right place for two white guys from the boats to hang around for long. Gary could be a dangerous place; there were still many unresolved tensions in the seventies. We had heard stories of sailors who were beaten and robbed on their way back to the boats. We had been warned of deckhands who were shot at, whose fingers were cut off to get at the rings they wore. But none of that crossed our minds as we strutted around the bar that night. The band never did let me play those drums. Lucky for us, George and I were too tired to walk back to the boat and called a taxi. And lucky for me, I still have ten fingers.

Although we drank our share, barhopping wasn't our only activity uptown. For some exercise and a diversion, we sometimes brought a football with us and found an empty school yard for a game. When we tied up in Chicago, a few of us caught the El train uptown to the Loop. We visited the Chicago Museum of Art, dined in some of the finer Italian restaurants, and shopped for Christmas gifts at Marshall Fields. Just being in the midst of all that hustle and bustle of holiday shopping in the Loop put us in a grand mood. Such a contrast of cultures. One minute we're dining in a fine Chicago restaurant, catered to and fussed over by waiters in white tuxedos; the next minute we're back on the boat pinning hatch covers in the rain with a drunken bosun in a yellow monkey suit. Maintaining your sanity. That's what it was all about.

My favorite bars, in name only, were in South Chicago. On a quiet Sunday afternoon, we dropped by a place called "Horseface Mary's" that was in a run-down, bare-bones neighborhood. When we approached the bar, the front door was locked even though we could see all the people inside drinking. A loud, raspy voice called out to us through the plate glass, "Push the Buzzer!" But before we could press the buzzer, a large vicious-looking German shepherd lunged at the glass doorway, barking and snarling menacingly at us. We were about ready to give up on the beer when someone called the dog off and let us in. We gulped down a quick Budweiser, bought a pint of brandy to take back to the boat, and eased our way out of there. With the slightest nod from Mary, that dog would have grabbed any troublemaker by the throat and put him flat on his back. I used to think some bouncers were intimidating until I met this little pooch. If this watering hole didn't quite measure up to our expectations, we could always head down the block and give "Peckerhead Kate's" a try. Just keep an eye out for the rottweiler.

Soundings

Before long, my prospects on the freighters began to look very appealing. After all, I could work eight or nine months a year and have my winters off. I would be guaranteed decent wages, paid unemployment, and plenty of time to read or write. The fleet of nearly fifty U.S. Steel vessels seemed to be thriving and almost ensured a secure future.

I thought of working my way "up the hawsepipe" from lowly deckhand to AB deckwatch, then to watchman, first mate, and someday captain. It was just a matter of serving time and passing the appropriate exam. It seemed like things were finally starting to fall into place for me. For the last several years, I had been searching for something exciting to pursue, a lifestyle that wouldn't grow stale with time. Perhaps I had found it.

Not a single decision we make ever occurs in a vacuum. The same could be said for the choices I made as a deckhand, against the social and political backdrop of the moment. Like my peers, I was a product of the times, stirred by the issues of the day. One small choice can influence so many of our decisions further down the road in ways we never quite realize. It's like a ripple effect. Think back, for example, about a particular choice to move to a specific neighborhood or city, or a new school to attend. Consequently, one meets new people and soon realizes that these new surroundings and personal relationships have an influence on us in countless ways. Opportunities present themselves that would have otherwise been missed. All because of some seemingly insignificant choices made long ago.

In the U.S., during the early seventies, we learned to live with the consequences of some unfortunate choices. America's system of politics-as-usual was collapsing. From the 1968 Democratic Convention and the violent protests in the streets of Chicago to the Watergate scandal and the Nixon administration, American culture had been stood on its head. The American public trusted neither the government nor the politicians to do what was right for us. Corruption was widespread, not only in the federal government, but throughout corporate America. The institutions of hard work, marriage, and higher authority were threatened. As part of the upheaval in society, we questioned everything, and we wanted some honest answers. Business as usual was no longer acceptable.

People no longer had faith in the Nixon administration. We had been ground down by the endless bloody war in Vietnam, by the anti-war protests on the streets of America, by the flag burning and draft card burning across the country. The Pentagon Papers revealed even more lies and deception by the government. Day by day, newspaper headlines trumpeted the latest from the unraveling and very disturbing Watergate scandal. The country was extremely divided by the politics of the Vietnam War — the hawks versus the doves, the anti-war Democrats against the pro-war Republicans. We didn't trust the authorities anymore and began to question other social institutions.

On board the ship, younger crew members wore shoulder-length hair, beards, and bell-bottom jeans. Some of the guys had sewn American flags on their jeans for patches. Now and then, the sweet smell of marijuana drifted through the tunnels below deck. Most of this did not sit well with older crew members. The bosun and mates saw all of it as disrespectful and rebellious, but there was little they could do. Signs of a culture clash were looming.

In January 1973, the Roe v. Wade Supreme Court decision was handed down legalizing abortion. More protests were staged across the country, pro-life versus pro-choice, dividing this country even further. People were dissatisfied with their dead-end careers, climbing the corporate ladder for the supposed wealth and prestige. We had basic cultural questions. How should we define success? Was it more material goods? A high-paying career? How could we improve on the traditional idea of marriage? In all corners of society, people were disillusioned with the present state of affairs and wanted better answers. It was a time for inner reflection and contemplation. Our choices would determine our future, both individually and as a country.

In many universities, students campaigned for a pass-fail system of grading so they could concentrate on the depth and meaning of each course rather than focus exclusively on the letter grade. They also demanded that more relevant classes be offered that pertained to their everyday lives. Overall, we wanted simpler, more practical lifestyles. On many campuses, Thoreau's "Walden" and Charles Reich's "The Greening of America" were widely popular. Thoreau had challenged, over a hundred years earlier, many of society's values including our so-called work ethic and our view of material goods. He believed that if we could limit our material needs, we could work fewer hours in the day, and, as a result, would lead simpler and fuller spiritual lives. We would have the time to pursue a higher calling. Reich chronicled the great social changes sweeping the country. He hailed many of the countercultural movements including challenges to corporate values and resistance to the military draft, as well as the drug and hippie lifestyle. The youth culture across America was demanding a slower, simpler, more sensible approach to life. Both

Reich and Thoreau believed in the free expression of liberated individuals, that man had a deep need to renew his relationship with himself, with society, and with nature. America was seeing itself through the fresh eyes of a new generation.

In such turbulent times, both politically and socially, quite a number of my fellow crew members seemed alienated from their jobs and from themselves. Typical sailors were too macho to talk about it in quite those terms, but they expressed themselves in other ways. A mate might mention that he really missed his wife and kids, that he regretted seeing them only a couple times a season, and wondered if his kids were basically growing up without a father. An engineer would brag reluctantly about his fifteen years of seniority and how he could retire with a pension in another twenty years; after that, he would really start living the life he had dreamed, traveling and perhaps starting a business of his own. Others literally counted the days until their next two-week summer vacation, a time of freedom and relaxation away from the confines of shipboard life. There was an overall tendency to live in the future instead of the present. The lives they wanted to lead were, in a sense, put on the shelf. Sometimes, it must have seemed hopelessly frustrating to them.

I wondered what on earth they were waiting for. Why didn't they simply quit and pursue something for which they really had a passion ? Did a steady income have to dictate their lives? At the time, I didn't realize that some of these men had families with growing kids, mortgages, and other obligations. They couldn't simply quit their jobs for selfish reasons and move on without any financial security.

As I look back now, it seems that a great many of us settle into a type of work we really haven't planned. A decent job comes along, we accept it, and before we know it, twenty years have flown by. Now we're married, we have kids, we have bills. Not so easy anymore to abruptly change direction. And that's the way life is. One decision influences another, the ripple effect. As long as we are aware of this connection, we can take time to consider all options before altering our course.

As this widespread search for self-identity and self-awareness grew, things everywhere were loosening up. Hippies were trying to "find themselves," waiting for life to strike a match and light the way. The drug culture blossomed and made available everything from marijuana, hashish, and LSD to uppers and downers. Everyone seemed to be getting high with Cheech and Chong, The Grateful Dead, and the Stones. "Right on," "far out," and "heavy" were the most common phrases one needed to communicate with the culture. Free love was offered in place of monogamy, having started back in the Haight-Ashbury district of San Francisco in the late sixties. During the height of the Vietnam War, the popular slogan was "Make Love, Not War." Everywhere, it was bell-bottoms and long hair up against the suits and the establishment, the status quo versus new solutions to society's problems. The youth culture overflowed with confidence and was quickly emerging as the mainstream of society.

The Nixon administration was disturbed and exasperated by the anti-war movement, by the chaos and the overall dismantling of society. National Guard troops were ordered to campuses around the country to quell disturbances such as draft card burning, war protests, and student takeovers of campus buildings. The turmoil culminated in the shooting deaths of several students on Ohio's Kent State campus in May of 1970. That event helped to galvanize the country against the increasingly unpopular Vietnam War and its mismanagement by the Nixon White House. As a country, we felt isolated by the wayward direction of our leaders, our institutions, and our society in general. We knew that we had lost our way and needed to chart a bold new course.

The search for more meaningful directions would lead to smaller work settings instead of the large corporate environment of the past. Art fairs sprang out of the need for a closer relationship between the producer of an object and its consumer. The fairs introduced simplicity and a human element to everyday commerce. To get closer to nature, groups of people formed communes—living together and sharing the chores, child rearing, and food. This back-to-the-land movement inspired many hardy individuals to find farms and work to become more self-reliant. They wanted to be closer to nature, to have time to reflect and relax with their family and friends. Others hitchhiked across the country with no particular place in mind, searching for adventure, romance, or whatever came along. No cares, no worries. It was the opposite of traditional responsibility, a slap in the face to rigid authority. And, for many, it was exhilarating and enlightening. Altogether, it served as a retreat from the obsessions and addictions of wealth, power, sports, and material goods to which America had surrendered. This movement reaffirmed the importance of meaningful work and a simpler life. It challenged hierarchies and blind authorities that had given us such dismal guidance and such poor advice on how we ought to live our lives and what we ought to value.

Day by day, I began sounding out my own positions while aboard ship. I was determined to set a fresh heading, to chart a bold new direction for myself. And yet, I was distracted by the confusion and uncertainty of the times. So inspiring and idealistic one moment, so demoralizing and dispiriting the next. I would have to bide my time and wait for something to unfold.

⚓ ⚓ ⚓

How many times must a man look up
before he can see the sky?
Yes, 'n' how many ears must one man have
before he can hear people cry?
Yes, 'n' how many deaths will it take till he knows
That too many people have died?
The answer, my friend, is blowin' in the wind,
The answer is blowin' in the wind.

--- Bob Dylan, "Blowin' In The Wind"

Standing Watch

The St. Mary's River is a beauty to behold. Its breathtaking islands and sparsely populated shorelines capture the imagination in a way that only nature can. From the Soo Locks downbound to Detour, about a five-hour passage, steamers wend their way through the Little Rapids Cut near the Sugar Island ferry, squeeze through the Rock Cut at Barbeau, cross the muddy waters of Lake Munuscong, and meander towards the Detour Reef Light. Summer sunrises are glorious as one listens to the chirping of the birds slowly awakening. A faint mist often hovers just above the river, slightly obscuring a few hopeful fishermen in their small boats. Posted on the ship's bow, taking all this in, is the watchman, whose job it is to keep an eye out for approaching traffic and hazards of any kind. The captain, mate, and wheelsman in the pilothouse are also keeping a lookout ahead, but it is the watchman's job to report anything first.

The Coast Guard requires a lookout to be posted on the bow whenever a ship is navigating through a river system or underway in foggy conditions. One sunny fall afternoon, the *Fraser* was making its way down the lower St. Mary's River. Standing watch on the bow was a fellow known as Squeaky. He was a squat, middle-aged guy from New Jersey who had a raspy, sputtering kind of voice that creaked and broke unevenly when he spoke, like a teenager entering puberty. In his off hours, all Squeaky ever talked about were the horses he played at the track and the gambling in Atlantic City. Damon Runyon's horse-track stories about the hard-luck gangsters on Broadway were his favorite. He could never get enough. He had a habit of squinting with a devious sort of Cheshire cat grin that reminded me of Danny DeVito in *One Flew Over The Cuckoo's Nest*. Well, Squeaky was keeping a lookout on the bow that afternoon, scanning the horizon with his binoculars as far downriver as he could see. The front window of the pilothouse was open to hear any communication from the watch. Suddenly, he turned and shouted very matter-of-factly, "Steamboat coming upriver, Cap. Two points off the port bow!" The traffic had been very quiet for the last hour, and we weren't expecting anybody. The captain and mate hustled over to the radar screen and carefully studied the area downriver and beyond. We were in a narrow part of the channel and couldn't afford to be out of position if another vessel was approaching. There wasn't much room to maneuver. Finally, the old man stuck his head out

Irving S. Olds and two other U.S. Steel steamboats down-bound at the Soo Locks; 1973. (Courtesy of U.S. Army Corps of Engineers/Soo Area Office photo)

the front window and scolded, "That's not a fucking steamboat, Squeaky, it's a goddamned island!" The watchman shrugged sheepishly and went back to studying the river.

At night, crossing the lakes or cruising through the rivers, the entire ship is fairly quiet. The only sounds to be heard are the muffled grinding of the massive engine strokes, the churning of the giant propeller, and the gusting wind from out on deck. Before waking the next watch, the deckwatch makes his usual rounds. His cleaning stations come first, sweeping and mopping out the hallways between cabins, collecting trash, running up the flag on the stern at sunrise. Back in the galley, the watch makes fresh coffee for the next shift.

Once in awhile, as the four-to-eight deckwatch, I had to take it upon myself to clear out the cold cuts in the cooler. The cook apparently didn't want to waste good food. So he tried to get as much mileage out of the cold cuts as possible. The cooler was stocked with lettuce, sliced tomatoes, onions, mayonnaise, and a variety of cold cuts from salami and pimento-loaf to bologna and leftover roast beef. The food was there for the crew if they wanted something between regular meals. For several days, some of the crew had been complaining about the green bologna and the mildewed lunchmeat; it was all starting to look and smell a bit rancid. There was nobody around while I was making the coffee, so I quickly grabbed the metal trays of meat and heaved them over the side. I also gathered up all the stale pastries and rolls off the crew's mess table and tossed them into the dark waters. It felt very satisfying to take matters into my own hands. The flock of seagulls that accompanied us on most trips across the lake was quite thankful for my generosity. The gulls usually perched themselves on number seventeen or eighteen hatch in a long chorus line, doing a hasty sidestep to either port or starboard to escape anyone approaching them on deck. When they saw the bountiful buffet I was offering them, the seagulls soared overhead, circled, and dove into the waves for an early breakfast. Later that morning, the cook was very disgusted that he had to serve up new cold cuts, but the crew was happy that justice had been served.

At six bells (7 a.m.), the deckwatch would wake the crew on the forward end for the eight-to-twelve watch, including the bosun, third mate, deckhands, watchman, and wheelsman. Most arose quickly and rarely needed a second call. The deckhands' cabins off the dunnage room below decks were small and not well ventilated. I opened their door, peered into the dark room, and hollered bright and chippery, "Rise and shine for the Pittsburgh line." If that didn't stir them, I tried, "Alright, drop your cocks and grab your socks. It's seven o'clock." Between the snoring and the farting, a wave of foul odor slapped me in the face and sent me reeling. I'm not quite sure what those deckhands had consumed at dinner the night before, but I thought for a moment that I was suffering from oxygen depletion. I learned to hold a handkerchief to my nose the next time I awoke them. They had about forty-five minutes to wash up, head back to the galley for breakfast, and prepare for the day. I had just enough time to sound the ballast tanks before eating my breakfast; then it was time to jump back in the rack for a snooze.

Once during each watch the deckwatch had to sound the eight ballast tanks on both port and starboard sides. The sounding rod was a rounded length of stainless steel about thirty inches long with an eye on one end and a heaving line tied to it. To sound, the deckwatch dried the end of the rod with a rag and chalked the length of it. After dropping it down the sounding hole on deck, he could read the wet chalk line to determine the amount of water in each tank. One drizzly November afternoon, we were crossing Lake Superior in some choppy weather, bound for Duluth. I was filling in temporarily as deckwatch and still learning my duties. The wind from the northwest was blowing about twenty knots and the whitecaps were breaking around us between eight to ten feet. When it was time to sound the tanks, I felt a little uneasy about walking down the deck with the waves so close to the gunnels. Our freeboard distance to the water was only about seven or eight feet. But I thought, *I may as well get it over with,* and marched tentatively towards the first sounding hole. I was about halfway down the deck when a wave broke over the gunnels and rolled over the tops of my boots. The icy cold took my breath away, and I grabbed onto the stanchion for support. At that moment, the pilothouse door swung open, and the first mate yelled down from the bridge, "Get the hell off the deck! You're gonna get washed over! Do your sounding in the tunnels!" I felt embarrassed at my stupidity but relieved that I could finish my job in the tunnels that ran below decks. A rogue wave could have easily swept me over the side, but in my ignorance, I thought the job had to come first. Thank God I wasn't forced to pay a greater price for my ignorance and inexperience. No one learns everything overnight, but sometimes I was just plain lucky to get away with foolishness. I was slowly working my way up the food chain.

Coming into port or locking through the Soo required certain preparations by the deckwatch. As soon as the mate let us know which lock we were assigned, I ran the steel mooring lines through the chocks and tied each one to a heaving line. When we were downbound, lines ran to the starboard side if we had the MacArthur Lock and to the port side if we were given the Poe Lock. Today, ships under eight hundred feet in length can use the MacArthur, but thousand-footers must lock through the Poe.

It was important to tie a good slip knot from the heaving line to the eye of the mooring line, rather than a half hitch or granny, so the deckhands could give it a good yank with one hand to free it up. Also, the heaving lines had to be coiled just so, free of "assholes," or kinks in the line. Otherwise, they wouldn't lay out properly when tossed to the waiting deckhands on the dock.

If the *Fraser* locked through at three in the morning, a line handler usually met us at the end of the pier. He assisted the deckhands being swung down on the bosun's chair. Some mornings the line handler fell asleep in his little shack at the end of the pier. We'd have two deckhands landed and be walking the boat into the lock when the sleepy guy would come running out of his little house, startled that we had sneaked right past him. Rubbing his eyes, he would often call up to someone near the galley to throw him down a quart of milk for his cereal and a couple of oranges if we could spare them. Talk about balls.

If we were coming into port, the deckwatch rigged up the boarding ladder back aft and the parcel bag as well. Any packages or loose material had to be raised or lowered in the parcel bag because two hands on the rails were needed to climb up or down the boarding ladder. A steel platform was hung from the ship's rail next to the ladder for getting on and off. Leaving port one time, Red, the deckwatch, raised the ladder without removing the platform. As the ladder ascended, it caught the edge of the platform, lifted it off the rail, and dumped it in the harbor. The boat drifted away from the dock as Red stared at the bubbles from the sinking platform. He knew that the bosun would chew his ass for this and disappeared quickly up the deck. When Dirty Dan discovered the platform was missing, he went looking for the deckwatch. "Where's Red?" he demanded. "Down in his room," another deckhand said, "He says you're gonna can his ass, so he's packing his bags for the Soo." Luckily, Red survived that one, all two hundred and eighty pounds of him.

Every Wednesday, after supper, the cook and porter handed out fresh linen to the crew. Clean sheets, towels, and pillow cases. On Thursdays, if the weather on the lake was decent, we carried out fire and lifeboat drills. The ship's whistle sounded and everyone donned his life jacket, scrambled to the main deck, and manned his assigned fire station. Canvas hoses were unrolled, hooked up to the water mains, and squirted in long streams over the side. At the sound of the next whistle, the crew hustled to the boat deck back aft to man the lifeboats. We uncovered the two lifeboats and cranked them out on the davits, but it was unnecessary to climb aboard them. The mates demanded more speed as we cranked, telling us it would be a race against time if the ship were going down. However, the crew had talked about this many times. Most of us believed there would never be enough time to scurry back to the lifeboats, unless we should sink under ideal conditions, which would not likely be the case. It would be quite difficult to launch a lifeboat in twenty-foot seas. The other possibilities were the two inflatable life rafts. But if we threw these rafts in the lake, we would have to jump into the frigid water and swim to the raft. In November or December, a person could die of either thermal shock or cardiac arrest upon hitting that icy lake water. So what good were our life jackets? We resigned ourselves to fate and didn't talk about it much. But we honored the mandatory Coast Guard regulations and carried out the drills anyway. Perhaps it gave us a faint sense of security.

Half Hitches and Granny Knots

All work and no play would be an awful way to spend the day. Some crews are very sober-minded, while others search for as much amusement and recreation as they can cram into a day. To keep our spirits up and to pass the time, we created diversions, pulled pranks, and kept our eyes open to the sillier sides of life on a freighter. Anything to keep us from brooding about our solitary lives on the lakes. Every ship was different in terms of what types of activities were allowed. But if it helped the crew's morale and nobody got hurt, it was generally ok.

On almost every ship, cribbage and poker were by far the most popular games. There was always a cribbage board and a deck of cards sitting around the dunnage room or back in the galley. Fifteen two, fifteen four, and a pair for six. We played a nickel a point or sometimes for beers if we each had a stash put away. Five-card stud took place every other night back in the officers' dining room. The betting sometimes got heavy, some guys losing several days' pay in one evening. Tempers flared occasionally, but no fistfights ever broke out. That would have been a sure way of ending a sailing career. Poker was too rich for the cribbage players' tastes, white-collar excess versus blue-collar common sense. Why work hard all day for a paycheck only to give it away at night? Most of the married guys sent their paychecks home to their wives to pay bills but kept enough cash handy to cover their vices. Draw days were on the tenth and twentieth of each month. Living on the ship, it wasn't hard to save a fair chunk of change. Not that there weren't temptations.

My first fall on the *Fraser,* someone had the idea of building a Ping-Pong table in the pipe room back aft. The engineers designed and constructed a heavy-duty iron-pipe base for the table while the deck crew built and painted the plywood top. For safety and heavy-weather precautions, the whole thing had to be drilled and screwed securely to the deck. Everyone participated in the project in some way. For all we knew, we may have had the only Ping-Pong table on the lakes, and we were mighty proud of it. The nightly poker games suddenly took a backseat to the hotly contested Ping-Pong matches. On nights when the ship was experiencing a slight roll from side to side, playing a game of Ping-Pong was like tap dancing on the Tilt-A-Whirl. Not impossible, but certainly a physical challenge. Late in the season when moods began to darken, this simple game brought out our competitive spirit and boosted everyone's morale.

Columbia Star, downbound in the Poe Lock; June 25, 2004. (Courtesy of U.S. Army Corps of Engineers/Soo Area Office – Carmen Paris)

On board the *Ralph Watson* the following summer, we received permission from the old man to play baseball on deck. One warm Sunday afternoon on Lake Huron, we brought out the softballs, gloves, and bats that one of the deckhands had scrounged up at a local Salvation Army store. Someone brought out a portable radio and cranked up the tunes. We played a game of five hundred; it was safer than running bases on a slippery deck. The batter perched himself atop hatch number one and drove soft grounders and pop-ups to several of the outfielders stationed near hatches number eight and ten. One bounce was fifty points, two bounces twenty-five points. No running was allowed; but if anyone wanted to dive, he was on his own. Some of the older guys came up on deck to watch; they just shook their heads and couldn't believe what they were seeing. One by one, the six softballs that we had started with took a funny bounce or a bad hop, leaped hopelessly over the railing, and floated away in the distance. Our impromptu game of five hundred lasted about twenty minutes or so, until the last ball skipped over the side. We needed a lemonade break anyway.

One summer in the mid-eighties, as a cadet from the Great Lakes Maritime Academy, I sailed aboard the thousand-footer *Columbia Star.* By that time, it seemed to me that every ship favored a particular sport or form of onboard recreation. On this ship, weight lifting was quite popular with the crew. It was a great way to tone up and an effective way of fighting off the pounds gained from sampling all the delicious pastries offered up every morning by the second cook.

One of the most surprising activities to see on a ship was bicycling. The *Columbia Star* boasted wide, unbroken walkways on her main deck that were perfect for cruising on a bicycle. Some of the older ships were constructed with raised plating on deck that was too easy to trip over if a crewman wasn't careful. Out in the middle of the lake, on a peaceful evening, several guys hopped on their bikes and rode laps from stem to stern. If the lake and the wind were calm, ten miles of riding wasn't out of the question.

What next? Roller blades and Razor scooters?

Another high-demand activity on the *Columbia Star* was watching movies after work on the VCR. Over the winter, one of the deckhands had taped hundreds of movies off cable and brought them aboard for everyone to enjoy. After dinner on some evenings, several of the engineers would get together for a game of Trivial Pursuit. They were such diehards about that game that it was difficult to keep up. They had an interesting way of rounding up players. One evening while I was out walking laps on the deck, a loud booming voice came over the deck speaker system: "Listen up! Listen up! Will Mr. Hill please report to the galley immediately for a game of Trivial Pursuit? Over and out." It sounded like the voice of God the way it thundered over the water. It was the second assistant engineer on the pilothouse mike. How could I refuse an offer like that?

For great summertime relaxation, it's hard to beat golfing on a Great Lakes freighter. The wide-open deck area between hatches was our green. A warm Sunday afternoon in the middle of Lake Michigan made for one of the finest driving ranges anywhere. Nothing but blue water and sunshine for three hundred and sixty degrees. The first assistant engineer brought up several buckets of balls, and we took turns driving them several hundred yards out over the lake. We even had our lemonade and chips. About the only thing missing was a barbecue grill full of sizzling steaks. Tiger Woods never had it so good.

Summertime on the Detroit River often brought out many of the large pleasure yachts with sunbathing beauties in their bikinis. Keeping a sharp lookout for them was the perfect spectator sport. In addition to navigating the river, those in the pilothouse kept a keen eye peeled for any girls in bikinis out soaking up the sun. It's no wonder that every sailor owns a good pair of binoculars. The lucky ones were the guys in the engine room. For a better view, they stationed themselves strategically near the gangway, a large open doorway into the engine room that was close to the water line. Sometimes the yachts would circle the ship several times as we made our way down the river. These beautiful women in their bikinis cruised close by the after end, smiling and waving to the lecherous crew hanging out the gangway. They knew they were every sailor's fantasy—tanned, stacked, and gorgeous. We wolfwhistled and beckoned them aboard, but they just smiled back and teased us. One time, a buxom blonde lying on the bow in her blue bikini sat up and whipped her top off. Swinging it over her head, she yelled over to us, "Hi boys! How do you like these?" And then the boat sped away. Girls gone wild; we loved it. Three of us nearly fell in the drink—willingly.

Things didn't always go as planned, especially when I tried to save a buck. One evening in Conneaut, towards dusk, I was returning to the ship by way of the dimly lighted railroad yard. One of the railway workers called me aside and asked if I wanted to buy some of his spiked apple juice for a dollar a gallon. He reached into one of the darkened railcars, grabbed a jug of his miracle juice, and gave me a sip. *Not bad,* I thought, *for a buck.* When I arrived at the boarding ladder, the watchman dropped the parcel bag down and hauled up my jug of hooch tightly wrapped in a brown grocery bag. To conceal it from the mate or anyone I might run into on deck, I went below and crept through the tunnel back to my room. I stashed it in my locker and forgot about it for several days. When I pulled it out to share with the other deckhands, we each took a long sip and spit it out across the room. My apple kickapoo juice had turned to straight vinegar. Great for washing windows or cleaning coffeepots. That was the last time I ever did business with any shady characters in a rail yard.

For sheer magic, one of the finest events of the season was the annual Thanksgiving Day feast. The entire crew looked forward to it for several weeks every November. As luck would have it, the *Leon Fraser* happened to be in Conneaut unloading when the big day rolled around. The crew's mood was very lighthearted in anticipation of not only a great meal but also a chance to go uptown afterwards. Floyd, the chief cook, took great pride in preparing this feast for thirty guys away from home. Thanksgiving, he knew, would bring back past memories of family and friends gathering around the kitchen table. Crew members would miss their wives and kids more on this day than they did all year long. He would give them a meal to remember.

The crew's mess room was decorated with orange cardboard pumpkins, golden horns of plenty, and crimson fall leaves. The Formica table was covered with white linen tablecloths, and each place was set with silverware, a white porcelain plate, and a linen napkin. Orange and yellow candles and a few bowls of mixed nuts trimmed out the rest of the table. The mouthwatering aroma of roast turkey drifted about the deck all afternoon. Most of us had cut back on our lunch and breakfast to make room for the big one.

At last, dinnertime arrived. We filed into the mess room and sat down elbow-to-elbow, cleaned and scrubbed and ready for some serious feasting. Bill, the porter, took each man's order individually and hurried off to the galley to fill it. While we waited, we studied the menu and wondered if we could try everything on the menu at least once and still have room for dessert. Soon the porter returned with plates piled high with roast turkey, roast duck, raisin and walnut dressing, sliced ham with pineapples and cherries, mashed potatoes smothered in gravy, buttered corn, cranberries, steamed carrots, candied yams, buttered squash, hot home-baked rolls, and tossed salad with three kinds of dressing. For dessert, there was pumpkin pie and whipped cream, cherry torts, and bread putting. We were absolutely overwhelmed. To top it off, each man received a cigar and a pack of unfiltered Camel cigarettes. We waddled up the deck to play a game of cards and groaned contentedly for an hour while we digested the whole gluttonous experience.

After awhile, we wandered up the street to Shaky Eddy's Bar to have a brew and to make our Thanksgiving phone calls to our loved ones and friends back home. It was a splendid finish to a fine holiday feast. Floyd had really outdone himself again.

We may live without poetry, music and art;
We may live without conscience and live without heart;
We may live without friends; we may live without books;
But civilized man cannot live without cooks
---Owen Meredith, "Lucile": Part 1, Canto 2

November Storms

The month of November is notorious for its violent storms on the Great Lakes. More ships have been lost in November than at any other time of the year. With all the sophisticated state-of-the-art weather-forecasting equipment that is available to ships on the lakes, the storms seem quite predictable. But all it takes is a slight miscalculation or oversight, and if a ship is in the wrong place at the wrong time, the lakes will find a way to claim another victim.

The fall of 1971 was my first experience sailing in rough November seas. One morning on the western end of Lake Superior, I was headed back to the galley for breakfast. I wore my long underwear, turtleneck sweater, chuke pulled down low, and a Carhartt coat buttoned up to my chin. The gray sky hung low and made the choppy water appear green and ominous. The four-to-six-foot waves seemed tolerable, and the light northerly wind barely caught my attention. The slight rolling motion of the ship helped me nurse my eggs and pancakes. It was a good morning to crawl back in the rack and catch a few winks, but that wasn't going to happen. Dirty Dan was waiting up forward to divvy up the work for the day.

By mid afternoon, things had changed considerably. We were heading on a northeasterly track, but the wind had shifted to the northwest and was gusting up to forty knots. The white-capped waves had increased to eighteen to twenty feet high with spray coming over the pilothouse. No one was allowed on deck. We tried to do our painting in one of the lockers below deck, but even that was getting to be a challenge with the constant rolling motion. The higher one is on the ship, the more noticeable the rolling effect. So we knew they were having quite a ride in the wheelhouse. Rather than getting pounded all afternoon on the port side, the captain had redirected our course to the lee side of Isle Royale. We could anchor there for a while and ride out the rest of this storm.

The first time I saw waves of this size, I simply couldn't believe my eyes. The enormity and the magnificence of Lake Superior is one thing, but seeing a twenty-foot-high wall of icy green water rushing at me was as frightening as it was spellbinding. First I felt like I was watching a movie and just enjoying the beauty of it all; then I realized this indestructible six-hundred-foot ship was nothing but a helpless tin bucket tossing around in a tempest. The ship could snap at any moment or dive under the waves and never come up. I soon realized that it wasn't at all

D.M. Clemson crossing Lake Erie in rough weather, November 1973. (Courtesy of the photographer, Fred Hill)

healthy to dwell on such matters. Although the ship was certainly vulnerable up to a point, she was designed to withstand the rigors of stormy November seas. In fact, standing up forward and looking down the deck toward the smokestack on the stern, I noticed that the entire steel hull structure definitely flexed like a big rubber pencil. *Bend,* I thought, *but please don't break.*

One could hear the groaning of steel on steel as the massive hull plates stretched and contracted. Within a few hours, we reached the protection of Isle Royale and dropped anchor there until the following morning. Companies don't make any money when the ships aren't moving, but their bread and butter also depends on the safety of the crew. The worst thing for a ship and crew is to be so far out into the middle of Lake Superior in the midst of a bad storm that there is no place to hide, no island or peninsula to offer shelter. By that time, one is strictly at the mercy of the seas.

In the late fall, as bad weather approached, the first mate would send word out to secure everything on board. Anything that was loose or not tied down was a potential accident. I once had all the dresser drawers in my room fly open in the middle of the night during a heavy roll, spilling the contents across the room. All hands knew to dress properly for the weather. If not, they'd be sorry. In late November, most of us were decked out in Sorel boots with thick felt liners, insulated goose-down jackets or one-piece snowmobile suits, balaclava face masks, heavy chukes, and leather choppers. With the spray sweeping over the decks and freezing, we had to be very careful of our footing at all times. We dusted the walkways with sand and salt regularly.

In the summertime, the bosun allowed us to tighten every other hatch clamp due to the normal mild weather. That saved us plenty of unnecessary work, considering the hundreds of clamps that needed to be secured. But when late fall weather rolled around, the mate insisted on clamping every single one of them to be sure that the hatches were watertight. If it was necessary to go aft during rough weather, we walked through the tunnels that ran below deck on

Early winter, *Paul R. Tregurtha* taking on supplies from the *Ojibway* just below the Soo Locks. (Courtesy of the photographer, Fred Hill)

either side of the ship. Some of the older ships still used lifelines that a seaman attached to his waist, the other end of it secured to a steel cable that stretched the length of the deck. This prevented the man from being swept overboard.

Late in the season, snow squalls often formed unexpectedly, blinding us with a blizzard of lake-effect snow. When cold winds travel across large expanses of warmer lake water, they pick up water vapor which then freezes into snow. The squall would come on suddenly for about twenty minutes, a wind-driven wall of white freezing crystals, then end just as quickly. For those few minutes, we were lost in a howling white-out as if someone had shaken us up inside a Christmas snow globe. With the help of radar, we were able to pinpoint our position, as well as the location of any vessels in the vicinity.

During one of those storms that first year on the boats, shortly after Thanksgiving, I reluctantly recalled the sinking of the *Daniel J. Morrell* just five years earlier. The ship had gone down on northern Lake Huron on November 29, 1966, with the loss of twenty-eight lives. Dennis Hale, the lone survivor, had clung to a life raft for many hours in the icy water before being rescued. It was nothing short of a miracle considering the hypothermic conditions he endured and the long freezing hours he had spent in the water. For a moment, the whole thing seemed surreal to me. Here we were, thirty men tossing around wildly in a Lake Superior gale, a very fragile existence that could be yanked away at any moment but for the whim of fickle nature. As strong as I felt individually and as indestructible as a giant ore freighter appears, yet I still felt vulnerable. We were at the complete mercy of nature.

The more I worried about my predicament, the more anxious I became. Then I realized that the lives of all people hung by a thread in one way or another. Accidents are waiting to happen, serious illness might attack us at any time, an assault could be coming around the next corner. It's not only impossible, it's downright foolish to live with this kind of perpetual fear and hyper-awareness. By the same token, sailors don't try to put themselves in harm's way any more

View from pilothouse of the *Columbia Star*, crossing Lake
Michigan taking a wave over the bow, 1986.
(From personal collection)

than the next person. They have the same fears, the
same respect for hazardous conditions. Sailors, like
others, learn to deal with unpleasant circumstances
as they come. The best we can do is to learn to relax
and trust that most matters will take care of themselves. We can be vigilant yet confident that our luck
will prevail.

I often wondered how Dennis Hale managed to get
through his grueling ordeal in the icy water after his
ship sank. Survivor's guilt may have haunted him
inescapably, yet other memories fortified him. In later
interviews, Hale spoke of the sense of purpose, the
sense of family, that the crew provided him by living and working all season long with them. Despite

all the fears and misgivings about being away from home for long stretches of time, a sailor nevertheless valued the comradeship and direction that shipboard life afforded. November, more than any other season of the year, seemed to bring about a focus on family and loved ones. Perhaps we realized how much we had to lose. I learned to be more thankful for all the blessings in my life and tried to be less critical when things didn't work out my way.

Four years later, the 729-foot *Edmund Fitzgerald* sank in a ferocious storm on Lake Superior. Twenty-nine lives were lost on November 10, 1975, just northwest of Whitefish Bay. Suddenly, these freighters didn't seem so invincible. Nature demanded respect. After a lengthy investigation, the Coast Guard began to require survival suits on all Great Lakes vessels because that was the only way sailors could withstand the frigid lake waters late in the season. A life jacket, up to that point, would only aid in locating the body. In the years since, survival suits have added a significant measure of safety to Great Lakes sailing.

A Bone To Be Chewed

We often remember exactly where we were and what we were doing during certain catastrophic moments in our lives: the Kennedy assassination, the *Challenger* explosion, the 9/11 disaster. For me, the sinking of the *Edmund Fitzgerald,* just outside Whitefish Bay on the eastern end of Lake Superior had that effect.

I had been off the boats for a year, rambling around Ann Arbor, playing drums in several rock bands. The summer before the *Fitzgerald* sinking, I had returned to the Soo, seeking work as a carpenter's apprentice with the local union. My hopes for a job were high, but my luck was dwindling.

Sunday afternoon, November 9, 1975, had been an unusually balmy day near 60 degrees and sunny. Such a pleasant day, in fact, that a bunch of the neighborhood guys organized an impromptu touch football game down at the Lincoln School field. We were having a great game that day until my friend Randy threw me a long bomb on a right curl downfield. As

I ran full blast to catch up with the ball, a set of steel monkey bars jumped in my way and stopped me cold. I crumpled into a heap, went into shock, and couldn't move. It felt like I'd been body-slammed by Hulk Hogan and every bone in my body was busted. After an ambulance ride to emergency and a healthy shot of Darvon, I learned that I simply had multiple bruises and a fractured left collarbone. The beautiful weather that day had been a seductive diversion. It was due to change abruptly.

All the next day, November 10, I was limited to lying about the house in a drug-induced state, popping pain pills, watching and listening as this wild storm outside developed. Winds were clocked at 70 mph with gusts up to 90 mph. As I lay on a water bed in an upstairs bedroom, I nervously kept my eye on the window glass on the west side that rattled so fiercely in its frame, I expected it to blow out of the wall at any moment. I turned on the local radio station, WSOO, to listen for any current news of the storm. Reports told of high winds that had driven water over the lock walls and gates at the Soo Locks that was now flooding the west end of Portage Avenue. At a number of retail businesses on Ashmun Street, the storm had shattered the large plate glass windows. With the high winds, the International Bridge to Canada and the Mackinac Bridge were forced to close at various times due to several vehicle accidents. Towering elm trees and mighty spruces had toppled all over town,

Edmund Fitzgerald lifeboat, on display in the museum ship *Valley Camp*, Sault Ste. Marie. (From personal collection)

collapsing quite a number of power lines and demolishing several cars. Garbage cans that had been put out at the curb the night before for morning pickup careened recklessly down the streets like runaway bowling balls.

The first news I heard that night of a Great Lakes freighter in distress was on the CBS Evening News. Walter Cronkite announced on his broadcast that he had a report from the U.S. Coast Guard that a large ore freighter named the *Edmund Fitzgerald* was battling a brutal storm with gale-force winds and waves as high as 25 feet on the eastern end of Lake Superior. Over the next hour, Captain Bernie Cooper of the steamer *Arthur Anderson,* which had been following about ten miles behind the battered

Fitzgerald, reported to the Coast Guard in the Soo that the *Fitz* had suddenly disappeared from his radar. The *Anderson* bravely circled the wreckage area for hours searching for survivors, but to no avail. By daylight, scattered debris was turning up on the Canadian shoreline: oars, life rafts, life jackets, and two severely damaged lifeboats.

It was truly an extraordinary moment to think that a ship this size could suddenly have slipped beneath the waves without so much as a distress call. Because of their massive size and structure, lake freighters seemed almost invincible. Who knew that nature could exact such a heavy price, that this ship was no match for her temperamental moods? In the days that followed, people across the Great Lakes region were stunned by this devastating tragedy. Gordon Lightfoot memorialized the sinking in his eerie ballad, "The Wreck of the Edmund Fitzgerald." It was a song that resonated deeply with a great many people, especially those who felt connected to the Great Lakes and the crews who sailed them.

⚓ ⚓ ⚓

There are numerous theories on what ultimately caused the sinking of the *Fitzgerald.* One theory proposes that she dove into a massive wave and could not recover, plunging her beneath the waves for good. Another theory speculates that she bottomed out near the Caribou Shoals area. This could have caused extensive hull damage to the ship; she then took on enough water to make her unstable in the pounding seas. A third proposal suggests that several vents and hatch clamps on the open deck loosened up enough to allow massive amounts of water to enter the ship.

Another point of view that hasn't been much discussed is what I call the "coat hanger" theory. Lake freighters are designed to withstand many of the twisting stresses and strains of Great Lakes storms. The hull plates flex and bend and absorb most of the motion forces in very severe weather. But there are limits beyond which fatal damage can occur. Crossing Lake Superior on November 10, 1975, the *Fitzgerald* experienced some of the most brutal forces of wind and water this big lake has ever delivered. Surely, such a severe twisting and bending of steel plates took its toll on the belabored ship. The intense pounding and battering the storm inflicted throughout the day may have weakened numerous hull plates in the same way that bending a simple metal coat hanger weakens the molecular structure enough that the bonds finally break. The joints may have simply been overstressed, deteriorated, and suddenly snapped in the frigid water. If the ship had taken on any additional water through deck malfunctions, this too would have acted as a catalyst to the stress and strain. Sometimes a seemingly insignificant detail can yield the most profound consequences. Ultimately, we will never know exactly what happened that night.

With no survivors, the mystery will always linger. As Lightfoot's song says, "The legend lives on ..."

⚓ ⚓ ⚓

We might ask who, if anyone, was at fault in this sinking of a once proud ore carrier. Who bears responsibility for a freighter being out in a storm of such enormous proportions? How could this have been prevented? Of course, one can always say that the captain of the ship makes that call. But the burden of responsibility rests with the steel companies that expect and encourage their ships' crews to keep moving up and down the lakes, often under foreboding circumstances. The deckcrews that I sailed with seemed to believe that captains are motivated to keep their ships underway, even in rough and unpredictable weather conditions, by some sort of year-end bonus. Anchoring too frequently is frowned upon. Companies make more profit by delivering their cargoes as swiftly as possible. These steel companies might want to issue a directive that ships are to anchor under certain hazardous weather conditions, whether current or anticipated, and not risk the lives of their crews. That would help eliminate the risky behavior of certain captains bent on burnishing their reputations by braving the elements and vicious weather conditions just to please their superiors by delivering their cargoes in a timely manner. Crew safety must always be considered, and certainly, with most ship captains, safety is always of prime importance. The *Fitzgerald* had a responsibility to find safe harbor that day. She may have pushed herself unwittingly into a tragic situation because, in the past, lake captains have sailed successfully through many a November storm. It was a calculated risk, a gamble against a tempestuous and unforgiving force of nature.

⚓ ⚓ ⚓

To this day, a ceremony is conducted annually on November 10 at the Great Lakes Shipwreck Museum at Whitefish Point to honor those lost in the *Fitzgerald* sinking. It is often attended by surviving family members and friends of the sailors who were lost. The only item recovered from the wreckage over 500 feet below Superior's surface was the ship's brass bell. On display now at the lighthouse museum, the bell was refurbished and engraved with the names of all 29 lost crew members. Every anniversary, the names of the sailors are read, and the bell is rung once for each of the 29 *Fitzgerald* sailors, and a thirtieth time for all mariners lost on the Great Lakes.

The *Fitzgerald's* two badly damaged lifeboats are currently on display in the Soo at the museum ship *Valley Camp*. The devastated hull plates and jagged metal bear witness to the destructive side of nature. The display is a stunning testament to the awesome power and fury of an angry Lake Superior one stormy November night.

⚓ ⚓ ⚓

Thirty-some years after this tragedy, safety precautions have certainly improved greatly on most of the lake freighters. With the advent of today's technology, weather reporting and communications have taken a giant leap in terms of quality and accuracy. The Global Positioning System (GPS), a satellite-based navigation system, and computers on board are able to pinpoint a vessel's exact location anywhere on the lakes. Survival suits are now standard issue on all Great Lakes ships. And yet, a ship's officers and crew must be ever vigilant. Overconfidence is the enemy of every sailor. A wise mariner develops a healthy respect for nature's capricious moods and unpredictable behavior. Just when we think we've got things figured out, Mother Nature shows us a new trick.

Wives and Girlfriends

Without someone waiting back home—a wife or a girlfriend—sailing would never be so sweet. A seaman needs a goal or motivation to keep going month after month, and knowing that a pretty woman is expecting him is reason enough. Some days nothing seems to go right. A guy may be as mad as hell at the world and want to just shove his job and head for shore. But he knows that a family depends on him or that his college tuition will never be paid if he quits early. So he cools off slowly and prepares for another day.

One of the toughest temptations for me to bear was simply locking through the Soo. In the summertime, my girlfriend, Judy, would run down to the Soo Locks to meet me for a few minutes as we locked through. We usually got the MacArthur Lock, the one nearest the tourist platforms, and I would be down on the dock walking the boat into the locks. On a warm July afternoon, Judy would show up by the fence looking as lovely as ever with her beautiful smile and a dark tan, wearing a bright pink halter top and white short-shorts. Her long auburn hair fell over her bare shoulders in a loose curl. I was lost in a dreamy trance until I heard the bosun's voice, "Hey! Wake up! Run that line down to the next bollard." While I waited for the water in the lock to drop down twenty-some feet, I had a few minutes to catch up on things with my girlfriend. I could feel the eyes of a hundred tourists as well as those behind me on the boat watching us. I wanted to reach through the fence and hug and kiss her passionately, but the Finn in me only allowed for a quick kiss and a few brief words. She said that when I got off the boats, she'd like to go skinny-dipping. Well, I nearly lost it right there. The mate hustled back from the Marine Post Office and summoned me back on the boat before we shoved off. I felt like Ulysses listening to the call of the sirens. I wanted to be tied to the mast so I wouldn't jump overboard and swim for shore. She looked so beautiful and inviting; how could I go back to painting and chipping? Within minutes, the whistle sounded, and we were leaving the lock. I waved to her and told her I'd see her next trip. As she walked along the fence waving up to me, my resolve to work the rest of the season nearly evaporated. I wasn't sure just how long I could last.

Other guys on the boat must have felt the same way. Horniness has a way of catching up to you. One morning, passing upbound through the locks, Harold, the wheelsman, sat on one of the hatches amidships

Supply boat *Ojibway* in the St. Mary's River ice; late December, 1999. (Courtesy of the photographer, Fred Hill)

with his trusty binoculars. A few of the others who were off watch sat nearby to scope out the female tourists who were also checking us out. Suddenly, Harold, with the binoculars glued to his eyes, found a raving beauty and shouted out for all to hear, "Holy shit! Look at the jugs on that babe!" The guys quickly scattered, leaving Harold to ogle by himself. What ever happened to the subtler, more disinterested style of checking out women? The casual but secretive glance at the thighs, the ass, the breasts, the hair, the face, the tan? All within a fleeting second before she catches him staring. Men have perfected the art. It was a sign: too much male companionship.

We were becoming an island unto ourselves. We had our tribal leaders, our peculiar language, and our own quirky customs. Everything may have seemed normal to us, but how did we appear to the rest of the so-called civilized world?

Below the locks we met the supply boat *Ojibway.* She brought us out fresh stores of food, salt and sand for the coming winter, and more paint to keep us busy. The *Ojibway* pulled alongside of us as we made our way down the St. Mary's River. For a few minutes, wives and girlfriends met with their husbands and boyfriends, often bringing a package of homemade chocolate chip cookies as well as news from home. There was little privacy for conversation, so most of the talk was everyday chitchat. I had once considered sneaking my girlfriend onboard the ship in a duffel bag, as part of our supply load. And I think she was willing. But I would have been forced to play bodyguard twenty-four hours a day, and the plan was abandoned. I realized then that making money had dropped down to second-priority status. I was in dire need of female attention. Nevertheless, it was always great to see friendly faces on the supply boat, if only for a short time.

No matter what the season, no matter what the time of day or night, a pair of walkie-talkies served as a lifeline for many couples. They were the maritime state-of-the-art for short-distance communication. Wives regularly met their husbands' downbound

Ralph H. Watson tied up in the Soo for the winter.
(Courtesy of the photographer, Fred Hill)

vessels at the head of the locks with walkie-talkies
in hand, telling of the latest happenings about town,
who got married or divorced, what activities the kids
were into lately. They walked the boat through the
locks, then drove down Portage Avenue and River-

side Drive, tracking the ship as far as Sugar Island to have a few moments of conversation with their hubbies. The walkie-talkie chase from one end to the other took about an hour. In that time, there was only so much you could say. Knowing they were being listened to by many sets of ears, the guys and their wives kept the conversation from getting too personal or intimate. A few walkie-talkie smooches and it was over and out until next week.

I remember a time when Judy came down to see me in the middle of the night. We were in the Poe Lock, the second one over, upbound in a swirling snowstorm. As we left the lock, she pulled up in a car and shouted to me through the blustery night, "Hi! I love you, and I miss you. When are you getting off?" Standing beneath a deck lamp so she could see me, I answered, "I love you, too." Being a Finlander, I was not ready to demonstrate my love and affection in front of the world. So that was all I could manage. The next day around the boat, rumor was that I was "pussy-whipped" and probably didn't have many days left onboard. I could hardly disagree.

In the summertime, mates and engineers often brought their wives, and sometimes their daughters aboard for a trip. One deckwatch started dating the first mate's daughter on a regular basis, and disappeared with her uptown whenever our ship docked in Conneaut to unload. The mate was possibly hoping for a future son-in-law. Another one of the mates had

The *Ralph H. Watson* being towed by a tug – that appears to be the *Edna G.* – into her berth at the Two Harbors ore loading docks. (Courtesy of W.A. Fisher Advertising & Printing; Virginia, MN)

a very good-looking seventeen-year-old daughter who liked to sunbathe atop the number three hatch. She wore a two-piece orange bikini, somewhat modest, and stretched out on a white beach towel. Hard to believe how many of us found a reason to pass by that particular hatch, if only to find another paintbrush, a scraper, or another pair of gloves. She, for her part, seemed to enjoy the traffic as well as the offers to rub lotion on her back.

There was also the story I'd heard on another ship of a mate's daughter who had disappeared for several hours one evening. They searched the boat high and low and finally discovered her tucked away in the lifeboat making love to the deckwatch. I think she was put under lock and key in the mate's quarters for the rest of the trip. The deckwatch was lucky to keep his job, one of the fringe benefits of union membership.

There's nothing quite so humbling as being humiliated in front of a crowd, especially for a shy person of Finnish descent. Passing downbound on another ship one afternoon, my brother Bill stood by the bosun as they entered the lock. The platforms were crowded with the usual tourists flashing pictures, observing the crew in the fishbowl. They asked the same questions every trip—where we were bound, what cargo we carried, and so on. My mother had come down to pay a visit to Bill, and had to shout to be heard over the clatter of the tourists. Waving wildly from the platform, she hollered out, "Bill! Bill! Do you have enough clean underwear?" Up on the boat, Bill could only smile and say to the bosun, "Who the hell is that lady over there?" Of course, the tourists found it very amusing to witness such loving concern over a son's personal hygiene.

⚓ ⚓ ⚓

Leaving one's family in the spring to fit out a boat was always quite difficult. My father-in-law, Joe, who worked for U.S. Steel for about sixteen years as a fireman, hated to separate from his family every March to fit the boat out in Lorain or Duluth. When they drove him to his destination, the family went with him, including Grandma and the dogs. They hugged and cried for a long time before he finally pulled away and climbed aboard the ship for another long season. On a number of occasions, he almost gave up sailing to find a job on shore and be with his family. But, in the end, he knew it would be foolish to throw his job security in the drink. A few weeks aboard ship and life would even out and not seem so hard. It was just a way of life that both he and the family adjusted to after a few years.

What made it more bearable were the letters from home every week or so. They offered a lifeline of support that made the shipping season shorter and sweeter. We usually picked up our mail in the Soo or from the mail boat in the Detroit River. Receiving pictures of the kids and family or a picture of a girlfriend in her bikini made all of us long for home, but at the same time let us know that we were not forgotten. On the *Ralph Watson* one summer before heading back to school, I had the opportunity to learn Morse code from the chief engineer. He had convinced me that learning the code would be an easy and inexpensive way of communicating with my girlfriend from Ann Arbor to the Soo. I could save a bundle on telephone calls. Once I learned the code, the chief helped me build a small Heathkit transmitter that I could take to my dorm. After Judy learned the code, I sent her letters in the form of Morse code on a cassette tape. We felt like CIA agents passing along top-secret information about foreign countries and nuclear weapons. When he saw me tapping out a letter in code, my roommate thought I had finally flipped out. He kept his distance after that, but I saw him whispering something to others. Although it seemed like a good idea at the time, the code soon became too burdensome to continue. And I missed the perfume and the lipstick that always accompanied her letters. Sometimes technology has to take a backseat.

As the season wore on, husbands and boyfriends seemed to grow hornier by the week, surviving on worn-out copies of *Playboy* and *Penthouse* to get them over the hump. The lucky ones, some of the mates and engineers, had conjugal visits from their wives. While we were in port, it was either a quick rendezvous at a hotel uptown or a brief tryst behind closed doors aboard ship. Anyone else would have to work his way up the street for relief.

As a cadet one summer on the *Columbia Star,* I joined several of my fellow crew members uptown one evening in the barrooms of Escanaba. We had a great time laughing and swapping sea stories, and before long, it was time to catch a taxi back to the boat. One of the engineers had invited his girlfriend back to the ship for a nightcap since we had about an hour or so before departure. Just before midnight, we arrived at the ladder to come aboard. But at the last second, we saw that the gangway to the engine room was wide open and only about a three-foot leap over the water. In our pie-eyed stupor, several of us, including the engineer and his girl, leaped into the gangway to save ourselves the climb up the ladder. Safety was the furthest thing from our minds. Once aboard, the engineer asked me to take his girlfriend up to his room where he would join her in a short while. The hallways and multiple decks on the ship confused me slightly in my foggy state, but I finally navigated my way through the maze and escorted the young lady to his cabin and said my good night.

A few minutes later, one of the oilers who was just getting off watch grabbed a baloney sandwich in the galley and headed up to his room. When he walked through the door, the first thing he saw was a pretty young woman lying on his bunk in nothing but bra and bikini underwear. She awoke suddenly and screamed. The oiler stared in disbelief, taking a deep pull on his cigarette. "What the fuck you doin' in here?" She jumped up, covering herself with a towel. "Ain't this the second engineer's room?" Whoops, I had put her in the wrong cabin. Those rooms were like hatch covers; after a while, they all looked alike. I felt as if I was in a Marx Brothers movie for a while, with Harpo chasing after a half-naked woman and me calmly calling for room service. We finally got everyone's feathers smoothed, and I returned to my room for a good cigar. Sometimes, when you step in it, you have to just scrape it off and keep on trucking.

Those are my principles, and if you don't like them . . . well, I have others.

---Groucho Marx

On Company Time

Every line of work is not strictly steak and po-tatoes; sometimes there's a good helping of fruit salad. We had our days of grimy disagreeable work, and then we had our share of gravy jobs. Late in the season, or when the weather outside was too miser-able for deck work, we were assigned jobs that even Martha Stewart would have killed for.

I still can't believe we got paid to do this, but it's true. After breakfast one morning in early December, the three deckhands and the deckwatch assembled in the dunnage room waiting to start the day's work. We knew that all the snowing and blowing outside meant some kind of inside work for the day. The bosun stumbled down the stairway from the deck carrying a large container of something mysterious in his arms. He told us to sit our butts down around the table, and then he placed the bowl in the middle. Reaching into the container, he handed each of us a nutcracker and revealed a large assortment of walnuts, pecans, and filberts. "Dig in, girls," he said, "The old man's wife wants fudge for the holidays, so start crackin'. This should keep you busy all morning." He scratched his ass, snickered approvingly, and scurried back up to his nest. We glanced at each other hesitantly, not sure if the bosun was trying to pull something on us. Then, reluctantly, four grown men in winter coats and chukes started cracking nuts with gusto. We nearly worked up a sweat by coffeetime. The second mate stopped by to check on us. With a look of pity, he smiled kindly, as if we were on the funny farm, and disappeared without a word. Before long, we got the hang of it and had the nuts all shelled by lunchtime. The only things missing were the tea and knitting needles. In the end, the cook made several pounds of fudge for the captain's wife, and the deck crew stayed gainfully employed.

Some mornings when the rainy fall weather made deck work impossible, the bosun simply told us to go change lightbulbs in the tunnels. That was code for "I don't want to see you guys until coffeetime." Changing a few burned-out bulbs in the dark tunnels that ran below deck required only a few minutes. For the duration of the morning, we found a place to sit down in the musty, dimly lit cavern and smoked and told stories. Two thin wire cables prevented us from falling thirty feet into the black empty cargo hold. I felt a little guilty sitting around doing nothing, but the guys said we had already paid our dues busting a gut on other jobs. "You got a problem? Are you some kind of company man or what?" they asked.

Waves pounded the sides and echoed across the hollow steel hold. We talked of our winter plans once the boat was laid up. One of the deckhands said he was thinking of buying a new Mustang and driving around picking up chicks. Another planned to hitchhike out to the Southwest to escape the cold weather. I considered hibernating for the winter with the help of a fat bank account and shipping out again in the spring. Before we knew it, coffeetime had arrived, and we reappeared on deck guilt-free.

As we got closer to Christmas, weather conditions restricted our work on deck. We still hosed down the deck with hot water after loading or unloading, tied the boat up in the Soo or in port, and finished up some minor indoor paint jobs. But for practical purposes, the brunt of the season's work was completed. Some days we sat in the dunnage room with new canvas and nylon line sewing our own seabags or repairing a torn coat.

As the holidays approached, we decorated the ship like a floating Christmas pageant. We stretched numerous strings of lights across the smokestack and mounted all of Santa's reindeer to the forward railing on the boat deck. In port one day, we ventured into the woods, chopped down several fir trees, and hauled them back to the boat. We planted them in two five-gallon buckets and set them in place on the captain's deck, wired securely to the railing. The crew decorated the trees with colorful lights, mounted a star on top, and even sang a round of "Jingle Bells." The bosun looked at us like we were getting light-headed and said, "C'mon girls. It's time for tea." Once the decorations were up, everybody's mood seemed to lift. It was looking more like home again. We awoke to snow-covered decks now and would spend a good part of the day shoveling a clear walkway along the deck. But a holiday mood was certainly settling in. There was even the occasional laugh from our grinch of a bosun. And if he could laugh, there was still hope.

Several other individuals on board found better ways to pass the long hours and make a buck for their efforts. Supply and demand. Find a need and fill the niche. Private enterprise, you might say, was alive and well aboard ship. Some of the mates, even though we considered them to be relatively well paid, started mail-order catalog businesses. If a wife's or kid's birthday was coming up and a crew member had no time and no place to shop, the mate could order him a brass barometer or a nautical music box and have it delivered to the ship within a few weeks.

One enterprising deckwatch kept a small refrigerator in his cabin stocked with Coke and Pepsi that his wife shipped to him on the supply boat every week in the Soo. He sold us pop and chips for a buck. He wasn't getting rich, but he enjoyed being a businessman.

One of the hardest working entrepreneurs was

Walt, the watchman. He was a burly, windburned fellow in his mid-forties who had learned the art of weaving nylon hammocks out of parted towlines. Somehow he had connections with several skippers and tug operators who sent him parted towlines, which he dismantled strand by strand and rewove into these wonderful, superstrong nylon hammocks. On sunny days when he was off watch, he worked on them out on deck. In bad weather, he set up shop in the windlass room and, like Rumpelstiltskin, spun this raw silk into a work of art. He sold the hammocks through mail-order ads in magazines and to many other sailors across the Great Lakes. Here was a fellow who not only made good use of his time but also loved what he was doing. I envied his enthusiasm and drive.

An oiler from back aft started a side business selling T-shirts and ball caps. He had them imprinted with the ship's insignia in various colors, and, of course, just about everyone had to buy one. Last I heard he was considering adding jackets and sweatshirts to the line. Never underestimate a man with time on his hands.

If there were a few extra hours in the day, pursuing a hobby was a great way to pass the time. According to some, the old man was fond of bird-watching. One day, in early December, we took on several sheets of plywood and some pine lumber on our way through the Soo. The bosun rolled out some blueprints and had us cutting out parts for what would be a giant purple-martin birdhouse. If that's what the old man wanted, then so be it. And we went to work with a gusto that even Santa's elves would have envied. Our small workshop was beneath the dunnage room, two levels below the main deck. Maneuvering the large plywood sheets and pine one-by-fours through the narrow stairwells was tricky business. Since there were no power saws on board, every piece was cut with handsaws. Each piece was handsanded and fitted. The deckhands, deckwatches, and watchmen worked on this project whenever we weren't busy with other deck duties. When it was finished after about three weeks of intense labor, this multilevel town house boasted twenty-two apartments, hand painted and freshly varnished. Some lucky purple martin would be able to comfortably house every friend and relative within fifty miles.

A few days before Christmas, while we were loading at the docks in Duluth, the bosun shouted down to me, "Hey, deckhand! Catch this!" And he proceeded to lower the oversized, handcrafted birdhouse by rope down to the dock. The last I saw, the bosun was strapping it to the roof of a taxi and headed for home. When I calculated the hundreds of man-hours that went into the construction of that glorified nest, I figured it cost roughly a couple thousand dollars to shelter our feathered friends. No wonder Dirty Dan was so enthusiastic about building that birdhouse;

we thought he was just brownnosing the captain. If idleness was the devil's workshop, then we wore our halos with pride and saved the company a bundle of trouble. At the same time, I'm sure that some smug purple martin family would be content living in the high-rent district.

Winter Sailing

After Christmas had come and gone that first year, the crew settled in for the final stretch—winter sailing. The coming days would be trying, if not brutal at times. Weather and ice conditions would become a twenty-four-hour obsession. As a navigation experiment run primarily by ships in the U.S. Steel Great Lakes Fleet, winter sailing lasted for an eight-year period from 1972 through 1979. Using innovative bubbler systems, U.S. Coast Guard icebreakers, and reinforced steel bow plates, these vessels attempted to battle the forces of Mother Nature through the grueling month of January and, sometimes, early February.

I had left the ship for a brief period to take care of some important school matters; when I returned in early January, the first thing I noticed was that everyone had gained several new layers of winter clothing. From their balaclavas and heavy chukes to their long underwear, sweaters, and snowmobile suits, all the way down to their thermal boots and leather choppers, this crew was dressed for the harshest winter weather the Great Lakes could deliver.

Things we had taken for granted in warmer times—like climbing up and down the ship's ladder, walking down the deck, handling lines on the dock—were now risky everyday maneuvers. One slip and a guy could be in the lake with cardiac arrest. After heavy snows in the upper lakes region, the deck crew shoveled for several hours to clear a pathway fore and aft. Although the decks were sanded and salted as necessary, we had to always watch our steps, keeping our hands free, never in our coat pockets. Anyone who has spent a few winters in the Midwest knows how unpredictable this season can be. Winter, they say, is not something to be afraid of or cursed, but should be accepted, managed, and welcomed. As long as one is dressed properly and not in any big hurry, the slower and simpler pace at this time of year can be fully enjoyed.

As January wore on, massive fields of ice formed in the St. Mary's River, in the approach to the Soo Locks, and in Whitefish Bay on the eastern end of Lake Superior. Whenever possible, several ships lined up as a convoy to make their way through the bay and river system with the help of the *Mackinaw,* the Coast Guard icebreaker that was assigned to aid vessels in winter navigation. The worst ice conditions could not stop the powerful *Mackinaw,* a 1944 vintage design with an invincible reputation. Leaving the locks upbound one day, the *Fraser* was under way

Wilfred Sykes and ice-covered *Cadillac* locking through the Soo in early winter (Courtesy of the photographer, Fred Hill)

for about ten minutes when she encountered a very stubborn mass of ice in the upper river. Following the half-frozen path of a previous vessel, we began to struggle slowly and finally grounded to a sudden halt. The captain backed her up a bit, cranked up the engine speed, and charged into the ice field again, but to no avail. We radioed the Coast Guard for assistance, and, in a short time, the *Mackinaw* came to our rescue. She measured two hundred and ninety feet long with a seventy-four-foot beam and looked impressive in her red-painted hull against the white field of ice. She raced to us like a Red Cross vehicle trying to save a wounded soldier. First the *Mackinaw* came along our starboard side, then passed us, and lunged full ahead into the massive ice ridges. The

147

powerful engines of the icebreaker thrust the bow slightly atop the frozen ice jam, breaking the mass with the weight of the vessel. She churned ahead for a couple of hundred yards until she had reached a thinner layer of ice. She then retreated and allowed us to continue our uncertain journey.

Winter was the only time of year when a deckhand might wish he had secured a job in the engine room. Not only was it a warmer place to work, but also sleeping was so much easier. The deck crew slept in cabins on the bow, just above the waterline. So every minute we spent plowing through the ice fields, the relentless pounding of ice on steel outside our rooms was deafening. At night, lying on my bunk, I would close my eyes and try to rest while the sound of a thousand hammers beating on the steel hull drove me mad. Sometimes, after a long while, the pounding became a sort of white noise, and I started to drift away only to be jolted awake by the sudden striking of thicker ice. When I couldn't stand it any longer, I wandered back to the galley for coffee and some peace and quiet. I would have to catch up on my sleep the following night out on the lake.

Traveling westward across Superior, we seemed to be picking up a lot of spray from waves off the bow. The *Fraser* was bound for Two Harbors, Minnesota, late in January for another load of taconite. The spray off the bow began to accumulate over several hours, coating the first five or six hatch covers with about

Columbia Star, downbound in the Poe Lock; January 14, 2004. (Courtesy of U.S. Army Corps of Engineers/Soo Area Office – Carmen Paris)

eight inches of ice. Within two hours of port, the wind let up a bit, and the captain ordered every available deck crew member to grab fire axes and start chopping the ice off the hatch covers. For over an hour, six of us chopped like mad but didn't seem to be making much headway considering the thickness of the ice and the massive size of the hatches. The mate then ordered the hot-water hoses to be broken out. That added a nice polish to the surface but didn't seem to affect the ice. It was late in the day, and the light was fading. As we approached Two Harbors, the mercury read thirty-eight degrees below zero. Finally, the captain came on deck and told us to knock off, that we would pull into port and wait until morning to load; besides, the ore chutes were frozen in place at the dock and would have to be freed up. Everyone's eyebrows, moustaches, and beards were coated with a thick layer of hoarfrost, and our limbs felt frostbitten. The men looked like Antarctic explorers from Shackleton's stranded crew. We were so relieved to go below and warm up for awhile.

The snowstorm that hit Two Harbors dumped eighteen inches of powder that had drifted most of the roads completely closed. Landing deckhands on the snow-covered docks in below zero weather was a little dicey, but we managed to get tied up without incident. Since the loading chutes were frozen and inoperable until the weather warmed up, some of us decided to grab a taxi and head uptown for a beer. Although there were no taxis or other vehicles moving about, a couple of guys on snowmobiles found six of us struggling in waist-deep snow to get to the bar. They shuttled us up the street in pairs to the American Legion and even offered to bring us back when we were good and ready. What great small-town hospitality on such a ruthless winter night.

When we awoke the next morning to start loading, Crazy Dog, the watchman, complained that he had a case of frostbite on his toes. The night before, at thirty-eight below, he had stood his twelve-to-four watch by the boarding ladder for safety reasons, running into the galley every so often for coffee. Even though he had the best winter clothing and the warmest thermal boots of anyone onboard, Crazy

Close-up of *Columbia Star* with ice-covered bow; January 14, 2004. (Courtesy of U.S. Army Corps of Engineers/Soo Area Office – Carmen Paris)

Dog wound up with frostbitten toes; they were turning colors and he had to get off at the Soo downbound. Meanwhile, someone else stood his watch, and I brought meals to his cabin to the total disgust of Dirty Dan. The bosun thought we were babying him and wanted nothing to do with it. For his part, Crazy milked the situation all the way to the Soo.

About six the following evening, the *Fraser* locked through the Soo without fanfare. At this time of the year, there were, of course, no tourists, no friends to come down to see us, only the dock personnel who stumbled reluctantly out of their warm-up shacks at the end of the pier to help us tie up the boat. The park fountain was covered with plywood sheets, the wooden benches wore a thick winter coat, and only a flock of pigeons flew by to welcome us. Due to darkness and the fact that two other freighters were not far behind us, the Coast Guard asked that we tie up below the lock wall and wait until morning to be escorted through the ice jams in the lower river. Just before my watch ended at eight that evening, the old man summoned me to the pilothouse to ask that I round up all the guys from the Soo. Captain Parsons had decided to offer us a belated Christmas gift and told the eight of us from the Soo that we were free to leave the ship for the night to visit our families. No watches to stand, just the agreement that we would return to the locks gate by 6:00 a.m. The guys were so overjoyed; they couldn't believe their luck. Within minutes, we headed into town for a surprise rendezvous. Two of my older brothers were also on board in the deck crew, and so we made a beeline for Hallesy's Bar to toast the evening. I went home for a short while, then down to Judy's house about ten and surprised the hell out of her. We stayed up all night after everyone had gone to bed, toasting champagne and getting intimately reacquainted. I felt like an old hound dog that's been out all night howling at the moon. Who cares about your bark or your bite when you can roam the night without a leash? But the next day, I had a hard time explaining all the hickeys.

By daybreak, the other two freighters had arrived at the locks for downbound passage. The three ships followed the icebreaker *Mackinaw* through the ice

Icebreaker *Mackinaw* leading *SS Canadoc* through ice in lower St. Mary's River; April 4, 1952. (Walter Materna collection, courtesy of Chippewa County Historical Society)

track of the lower river. Sometimes the ice that was locked through flowed downriver to the narrower choke points, such as Mission Point just below the locks and stacked up underwater six feet thick. This situation created problems not only for winter freighters but also for the *Sugar Islander* ferry, which crossed over to the mainland at this bottleneck point. Occasionally, the ferry became stranded by ice floes in the middle of the river and had to call for Coast Guard assistance.

About twenty miles below the Soo, near Barbeau, we approached the mouth of the Rock Cut, the narrow downbound channel between Neebish Island and the mainland. Neebish is an Indian word for "where the water boils," a reference to the wild rapids that once flowed through this area. In the early 1900s, the U.S. Army Corps of Engineers blasted a deep channel through the limestone rock and rapids to create another shipping channel. Throughout most of the season, upbound traffic runs along the east side of Neebish Island and downbound traffic through the Rock Cut on the west side. Depending on the severity of ice conditions, the freighters might run downbound through the Rock Cut well into January. At their discretion, the Coast Guard could reroute the downbound ships through the Middle Neebish Channel on the island's east side. In this initial year of winter navigation (January 1972), we weren't quite sure what to expect. As the *Fraser* slid through the ice-choked cut, the stone cliffs and piles of rock on either side appeared as lonely and desolate as the moon. For a moment, we were explorers on the lunar surface, the white glare all but blinding us in the mid-day sun. Without the icebreaker *Mackinaw* blazing a trail, there was not much chance of us making it through here safely.

Every spring, the Neebish Island residents are marooned on their island for anywhere from ten days to two weeks due to the thick sheets of brashy ice that float downriver, clogging the narrow confines of the Rock Cut. The islanders prepare for this isolation by stocking up on groceries and necessities in advance. Physically cut off from the rest of the world, there is nothing to do but wait. (At times, we might all be better off if we could withdraw to our castles, pull up the drawbridge, and leave the rest of the world behind for a while. A personal retreat for a fortnight. When we returned, we would be better rested and restored, ready for the wonders of a new season.) Nowadays, over the winter months, when the shipping season has ended, the island residents maintain a frozen ice trail from the island to Barbeau until the Coast Guard removes it just before spring breakout. The ferry then runs sporadically until the warmer weather flushes out all the troublesome winter ice.

Within five or six hours, the *Fraser* made it as far as Detour and hauled west for Lake Michigan. We passed through the Straits of Mackinac, a massive ice field that has damaged a number of vessels over the years despite the extra bow plates welded to their hulls. The winter navigation trail stretched east and west directly beneath the center of the bridge. As we approached the twin towers of the Mackinac Bridge, the stark beauty of this wintry icescape presented a magnificent sight. To the north, Mackinac Island in her isolated winter glory; ahead of us, Michigan's two peninsulas joined by a crystalline thread. We were witnessing the truly pristine solitude of Mother Nature at her best.

At the Soo, the captain had received orders to take our load to South Chicago and head to Milwaukee for winter layup. When the news spread around the ship that this was truly our final run, not another rumor, the crew was jubilant; we were headed for home. Any signs of grouchiness or bad humor quickly vanished. The deck crew would spend several days in Milwaukee buttoning things up, but many of the guys from the engine department would have to stay around for a couple of weeks to clean out the boilers and finish up some year-end maintenance. It was already the first week of February, yet many of my shipmates would be returning home to celebrate Christmas with their families. The year had been long and tiring for many, but the reunions would be sweet. The tree would still be up, lighted and decorated, with colorful presents beneath. This homecoming was long overdue.

There's a fire softly burning; supper's on the stove
But it's the light in your eyes that makes him warm
Hey, it's good to be back home again
Sometimes, this old farm feels like a long lost friend

---John Denver, "Back Home Again"

Hatch Farms and Fog Whistles

What's the difference between a fairy tale and a sea story? As any seaman will tell you, a fairy tale begins with "Once upon a time," and a sea story starts off with "Hey, this ain't no bullshit!" Over the course of a season, there are so many stories that circulate around the ship that you can't tell fact from fiction. There is often a fine line between the real story and pure bull, depending on the skill of the storyteller. To paraphrase Mark Twain, one should never let the facts stand in the way of a good story. As for sea stories, there are only three kinds: drinking, sailing, and chasing women. Not that the crew never talked about politics, the stock market, or music; it's just that these things seemed far removed from our watery world. Such conversations weren't nearly as entertaining as other concerns that were closer to home.

In the summer of 1972, I sailed on the *Ralph Watson* before heading down to school in Ann Arbor. It was a 1938 boat from the U.S. Steel fleet and had a good crew that made for a memorable season. Our bosun was a fellow from Sturgeon Falls, Wisconsin, by the name of Howard Olsen. He was a man of small stature, in his mid-sixties, who regularly wore a deadpan expression. It was hard to tell whether he was happy or pissed. Having sailed nearly fifty years, he was putting in his last season before retirement. Howard was generally a very agreeable and likeable man who had brief fits of temper whenever the deckhands screwed something up. Because he didn't drink and hardly ever swore, he stood out from the rest of the crew. He was such a far cry from Dirty Dan in terms of temperament and overall demeanor that it was a pleasure to work for him. By comparison, Dirty Dan made our lives miserable. When he got upset with us for something, Dan reminded me of that *Looney Tunes* character, Yosemite Sam, the way he threw his hat on the ground and stomped on it, jumping up and down all the while, cursing everything and everybody to eternal damnation. "Why, you highfalutin' varmint! I'll blow you to smithereens!" Howard, on the other hand, was more like Gary Cooper in *High Noon,* quiet and methodical, but determined to prevail. Howard always kept busy marching from one end of the boat to the other like he was on a secret mission of some sort; whether he was in search of a new paintbrush or a fresh pair of socks, we could never tell. This bosun never lost his temper unless we did something fairly stupid such as accidentally kicking over a gallon of paint on the carpeting in the first mate's quarters. If that had happened with Dirty

Dan, we would have run for cover fast because he would have erupted instantly. With him, it was like the running of the bulls at Pamplona: if you wanted to survive, you'd better run like hell, and stay two steps ahead of his lethal horns. He would gladly gore any deckhand within reach until the rage subsided. I think he saw me as the matador, always waving a red cape tauntingly in front of him. With Howard, we always got the day's work done, but felt like we were sailing on a pleasure cruise.

To get a job on the boats some years, it was necessary to accept a temporary assignment, with the hope that it might become permanent. In April of 1974, I was fortunate enough to get a temporary berth on the *Eugene Buffington* because one of the deckhands got off to have a tooth pulled. Little did I know what surprises were waiting for me. The *Buffington* was a so-called hatch arm, built in 1908, with heavy black tarps that covered the telescopic hatches. Up to this point, I was used to the iron deckhand that simply lifted each hatch cover and lowered it down between the hatch openings. That was pure luxury compared to the complexities of a hatch farm. My second day on the *Buffington,* we approached Lorain about 5:30 a.m. with a brief glimpse of morning light that turned quickly to dark, overhanging storm clouds. They soon broke loose, lashing us with a torrent of rain and pelting us with forty-mile-an-hour winds. In the middle of it all, the other two deckhands and I, with help from the bosun, loosened the clamps, pounded out the wooden pegs, and removed the sideboards to expose the tarps. Then we crawled across each hatch, four men abreast, on our hands and knees, rolling the stiff canvas tarp as we went. The pace was fast in the driving rain, and I had a difficult time keeping up. In our rubber rain suits, after two hours of rolling tarps, we were soaked to the skin from either rain or sweat, I wasn't sure. Then, to open the telescopic hatches, we ran a cable down the deck from an electric winch, through a steel eye, and hooked it to a cleat in the middle of the hatch to force it open. It seemed almost primitive compared to the other boats I'd worked on. After another hour and a half of freezing wet and cold, we finished our job and eased into port, only to be met by a brief hailstorm. The day was just beginning, but I was ready to crawl back in bed.

I shared my cabin, about ten feet square, with three other guys. No more than two of us could stand up to dress at the same time. Much too crowded for comfort, let alone any privacy. Living in such tight quarters made me feel like we were working on a cramped submarine crossing the Atlantic in search of German U-boats. A periscope might have eased my claustrophobia.

Around mid-May, we finally received word that all tarps on U.S. Steel's Great Lakes hatch farms could be removed from May 15 to September 15, the milder part of the season. What a great relief this was, a vir-

The *Eugene Buffington*, downbound in the early spring, approaching the Soo Locks. (Photo by Elmer Eckroad, courtesy of Chippewa County Historical Society)

tual four-month vacation for the deck crew. Another deckhand had told me that anyone who works on a hatch farm earns every damned penny; he wasn't joking. This was a working boat, not a gravy job; no question about it. I knew there was a god when the other deckhand returned from the dentist about two weeks later, allowing me to escape life on the chain gang. I felt as though I had somehow paid my debt to society, and I hoped to never again set foot on a hatch farm as long as I sailed.

About this time, I learned that the use of boat whistles to call for a lock at the Soo would be discontinued. Instead of the customary blowing of two long and two short whistles to request a lock, a ship would now be required to radio the lockmaster in the watchtower. Only the three long blasts for a fog whistle and the one short blast when leaving a lock would be retained. Growing up in the Soo, I remembered hearing steamboat whistles all night long on the river. They always reminded me of the endless parade of ships on the waterfront and of an adventurous life right outside my door. I'm sure the steam whistles kept many of the tourists awake at night in their motel rooms on Portage Avenue. But for me, the muffled sounds were not so distracting as they were reassuring, fading peacefully into the night.

All freighters under way in foggy conditions were required to blow three long blasts every minute to warn any nearby vessels. There have been far too many collisions in the past during foggy weather in which vessels didn't see each other until the last minute, when it was too late to avoid a disaster. Of course, the developments of radar and radio beacons have had a tremendous effect on ship safety. Aside from the safety issue, trying to work or sleep on a boat with the fog whistle blowing three times every minute was nearly impossible. When I walked down the deck towards the after end, the whistle would nearly blow me out of my boots and leave my ears ringing. Sleeping on the forward end, the mates and deck crew did not have it anywhere near as bad as those poor suckers back aft. It was worse than living in a bell tower. The relentless blasting rattled their bones, and shook the plates in the galley cupboards. As one of the wipers put it, "I need that like I need a red-hot rivet pounded up my pecker!" There was no escape, no mercy but for better weather. There was not much sympathy from those on the forward end who, months earlier, had withstood the pounding and hammering of winter ice on the bow.

As spring turned to summer, I found myself decking on one of the slowest boats on the lakes, the *Henry Phipps*. One of the older vessels (1907), she was in a delicate state of health and in no particular hurry to get anywhere fast. She went about her business with resolve and dignity and paid no heed to the thoroughbreds around her. The *Phipps* deserved respect and admiration for her many loyal years of service.

When I joined the *Phipps* crew, it was again as a temporary, the work to last perhaps four days to a week. Within a couple of days, word was that my job might turn into a permanent one. It seemed that Bob, one of the deckhands, was despised by most of the deck crew not only for his lazy work habits but also because he was a shameless racist and a nonstop whiner. Nearly everything he said was either hostile or boastful. The crew planned to harass the hell out of him and ride him off. There was no reason for anyone to stick up for him. Bob was a fully loaded grenade waiting for someone to pull the pin.

After supper one night, down in the dunnage room, the bosun called out, "Alright, who's been powdering their feet in the shower and left it all over the deck?" Jerry, one of the deckwatches, looked around the room and said tauntingly, "Bob?" His temper had a short fuse, and that remark ignited him. Bob flared up and accused everyone of always blaming him for anything that went wrong. He glared at Dave, one of the deckhands, pointed his finger at him, and shouted, "You cocksucking, long-haired prick! You're the one who's always starting it!" Dave stood up from his chair and braced himself as Bob waved a clenched fist in his face. "Fuck you, you fat bastard!" said Dave. That's all it took. With a look of rage, Bob backed off quickly and raced up the stairs to the pilothouse in a panic, demanding to be let off in the Soo. The air was pretty tense for about an hour or so while Bob packed his bags, not saying a word to anyone. The mate soon offered me a permanent decking job, which I accepted. I felt a bit guilty for snatching Bob's job. Like a deathwatch, we had been waiting for him to expire so we could read the will and divvy up his possessions. Several months later, he returned to the *Phipps* as a wiper in the engine room. We couldn't believe our eyes. Apparently, all was forgiven if not forgotten. Nevertheless, we kept a watchful eye on him.

While Bob was gone, we picked up another deckhand, a black dude from Jackson, Mississippi. A very likeable guy, easy to talk to, Albert was a track star who had a great deal of athletic promise. He said he

Henry Phipps taking on supplies from the *Ojibway* in the St. Mary's River, May 1953. (Walter Materna collection, courtesy of Chippewa County Historical Society)

had a chance to go to the Olympics in South America as a track and field man, but he turned it down because he needed the bread and decided to sail for a season on the lakes. Albert told us he could run the 440-yard dash in forty-six seconds. If that was true, we figured he was wasting a once-in-a-lifetime opportunity by working on the boats. On the other hand, his timing was perfect; if he'd have come aboard a few weeks earlier, he might have met Bob.

One of the more interesting characters we had on the *Phipps* was Doyle, the fireman, otherwise known as Mumbles. At the breakfast table, or down in the fire hole, he never stopped jabbering. Some internal conversation kept erupting from him nonstop. He was like a lost traveler, asking endless questions and answering them himself. What he was saying, we hadn't the slightest idea. It was a language from another planet, another species. We simply nodded to him politely and went back to work.

With nearly seventy seasons on the lakes, the *Henry Phipps* was a frail but proud senior citizen; however, the years had taken their toll on her. It seemed like every other trip, the stevedores punched holes in her side tanks while unloading the cargo. The damaged tanks, in turn, had to be welded and repaired. The ballast tank walls had apparently rusted thinner with age and could hardly withstand even the slightest bump from the stevedores' steel claws. Toward the middle of the summer, one of the boilers broke down as we headed upbound into Whitefish Bay. For twelve hours, we cruised at half speed until the engineers could fix the problem. But soon after, the boiler leaked again, and a major repair in Duluth was necessary. With the help of a highly skilled medical team, the precarious life of the patient was extended for a bit longer. She seemed to be running on life support. Rumors circulated around the ship that we were headed for dry dock in Superior, Wisconsin, but that never panned out. Like juicy gossip, rumors continued to fly that this would be the last year for the *Phipps;* she was headed for the boneyard. It was a shame that she couldn't become a museum ship somewhere and live out her twilight years in dignity.

The deck crew spent most of its time fighting the never-ending battle against rust and deterioration. Painting, chipping, scrubbing, and more painting. Yet Ray, the bosun on the *Phipps,* found time to be a Good Samaritan. Not all bosuns, I learned, were cast from the same mold as Dirty Dan. Some, like Ray, respected other people and had a sense of fairness about them. In Conneaut one day, the bosun rescued a pigeon from under the rusty loading rigs and brought him aboard in the mail bucket. The helpless bird was covered with a thick coat of oil that had dripped from the rig. After a bath, fresh water, and a meal of birdseed, the pigeon gained some trust in everyone but still couldn't fly. For several days, all the way to Duluth, he hopped about the forward deck, unable to fly very well, hiding under the winches when he grew tired. At the docks, the bosun turned him loose to rejoin his mates who were busy scrounging the area for food. With some gentle nursing and care, he had recovered to full health. For the bosun, watching the pigeon's flight over the water was its own reward. He knew he had done something small yet significant for a helpless creature.

In late July and August, the lower lakes turned un-bearably hot and humid. The muggy weather brought with it the hatching of millions of tiny flies about the size of well-fed mosquitoes. They tormented us night and day with their vicious bites. We couldn't hear them, but their bite was like the poke of a sewing needle. We tried to play cribbage after work, but the flies drove us insane. We fled up the stairs to the open deck, but they feasted on us like they might a raw porterhouse. Unless we retreated to the safety of our screen-doored cabins, our only defense was a flyswatter and a can of Black Flag spray. The intense summer heat seemed to drive the flies into a frenzy. We grew more anxious and aggravated by the hour trying to escape their relentless bite. And I had thought mosquitoes were bad; these were much worse by far. We could hardly wait to feel the cool relief of Lake Superior waters.

In the warmth of a late summer evening, the *Phipps* finally cast off her lines and hauled northward into Lake Michigan. When the deck was secured, we headed down to the dunnage room for a few shots of brandy before turning in. George swiped a can of orange juice and a pail of ice from the freezer back in the galley. Jerry brought out his Christian Brothers and Sunny Brook, and we toasted the end of a long day. Joe, the deckwatch, was the first to fall. All evening, Joe had sipped away at the bosun's bottle of Seagram's so that with a few finishing shots of brandy, he was in for a rough night. To make matters worse, he was just starting his twelve-to-four watch. The wind blew hard and warm rain pelted the deck as we plowed further into the blackness of Lake Michigan. The ship rolled easily side to side in the choppy swells. At midnight, Joe grabbed his sounding rod to head out on deck to sound the first four tanks. The engineers were pumping out to 0-20-30-40 inches on both port and starboard to give us a favorable trim in the choppy weather. Increasing the ballast water in the after tanks tended to make the stern of the ship ride lower in the water, thereby giving her more stable steering control. We soon realized that Joe was totally smashed, almost unconscious, as he stumbled up the stairs to the main deck to carry out his duties. With eyes at half-mast, he spoke like he had a mouthful of marbles. At first, it was a bit funny to us, but it was soon obvious that the weather was too dangerous for him to be out on deck; he could easily fall over the side in the storm. Of all people, Jerry, the deckwatch who couldn't care less what happened to anyone else, the guy who would never lift a finger for anybody unless he was popping them the flag, suggested that he and I take shifts sounding the boat until she was pumped out. We hailed Joe off the deck and made him sit down and relax. Jerry and I donned our rain gear and boots and off we went down the deck in turns. In the driving rain, it was next to impossible to read the chalk marks on the sounding rod, but we measured as best we could. Finally, we called up to the pilothouse to shut off all the pumps. Jerry volunteered to take the final sounding of the last three tanks; even with the rain coming down harder and the gusts picking up, he didn't shrink from the job. Joe sat behind the winch, watching Jerry work his way down the deck, and just shook his head in disbelief. He was dumbfounded that a guy like Jerry was helping him out. No extra pay, no promised favors. Gratis. Joe could have been fired that night if Jerry hadn't stepped in to help him. Soaked to the skin and still in a drunken stupor, Joe could hardly find the words to express his gratitude: "Tell him," Joe mumbled as he started to doze off, "Tell him . . . . he's all right." About three in the morning, we crawled into our bunks, exhausted but proud of the night's effort.

⚓ ⚓ ⚓

While we were usually more concerned with our own day-to-day affairs aboard ship, the crew could hardly ignore what was happening to this country politically in the summer of 1974. For many months, every television network and radio station, every major news magazine in the country, was reporting the riveting story of deep-rooted political corruption in the Nixon White House. The Watergate affair had caught up with the highest levels of the President's administration, and on August 9, 1974, President Nixon resigned from office. Like a ship trying to navigate in the fog, the Nixon White House had tried to steer its way through the haze of subpoenas and media accusations but had, at last, foundered. The moment was a classic watershed. With my shipmates,

I watched his farewell address on television in the galley. We all saw it coming. Nixon's reluctance to turn over the secret tapes, his repeated denials of wrongdoing despite the damning evidence, his many clashes with the Senate Watergate Committee. There was nowhere to run. So it was just as well he resigned, a fitting climax to many months worth of unfolding political drama; there was no need, at this point, to waste another two to three months impeaching and convicting him. It didn't matter whether the crew was Republican or Democrat; we all agreed that the country needed to move on. This was the first time in the history of the United States that the President had resigned from office, or more accurately, been driven out by his abuse of executive power. It was ironic that a man who had received the most popular support in presidential election history should be driven from office by public demand. As Nixon prepared to enter political exile, there seemed to be very little sympathy for him amongst the crew. The sullied president seemed to personify government corruption and pervasive distrust of many of our institutions. Like much of the American public, we wanted to put this sad chapter behind us and begin to heal this country's wounds. It was a great turning point for many of us personally and for the country as a whole. As Gerald Ford put it, "the national nightmare" was over.

"A patriot must always be ready to defend his country against his government."

---Edward Abbey

Maritime Discipline

With the passing of nearly a dozen years since my last trip on a Great Lakes freighter, my life had accelerated like a gale force wind. I had married, finished college, and started a new retail business. While I was living in Traverse City at the time, the lure of the lakes seemed to wash over me more frequently with every visit to the harbor. The sailboats, the blue waters of Grand Traverse Bay, the fresh lake breezes—it all began to stir my imagination and, in time, seemed to seduce me; it was time for a change. In the summer of 1985, I enrolled at the Great Lakes Maritime Academy at Northwestern Michigan College (NMC) in Traverse City. Studying for my First Class Pilot's license to become a mate on the lakes, I was taking full-time classes in a three-year program. I started school with high hopes that the program would eventually steer me towards a completely different life aboard the Great Lakes freighters. My classes that first year at the academy whirled by as briskly as the cool northerly breeze off the bay. In addition to studying seamanship, I also attended classes in physics, chemistry, and trigonometry on NMC's main campus. It was invigorating to be back on a college campus. Life was good.

For several years, my wife and I had run a successful crystal business in Traverse City's Cherryland Mall called "Forever Yours." Our small store carried various lines of Austrian crystal prisms and jewelry as well as pewter and crystal figurines. For a number of reasons, I had wanted to try something entirely different. Our lease at the mall was very short-term and gave us no sense of security. Even though the business was thriving, I felt trapped working inside such a plastic environment twelve hours a day; I wanted to be outside for a change, more in touch with nature. Setting store hours was not an option for us; the mall management set the hours, and we were bound to abide. So we opened the business seven days a week, twelve months a year, except for major holidays. Business was good, but we would eventually pay the price. Working too many hours, managing employees, and simply running a thriving business, slowly ground me down.

The (imagined) romance and adventure of the sailing life still pulled me. Once I got the hang of it, years earlier, I had enjoyed working as a deckhand despite the odd hours and the often-challenging bosuns. I knew what kind of conditions to expect working out on the lakes: a little sensory and cultural deprivation,

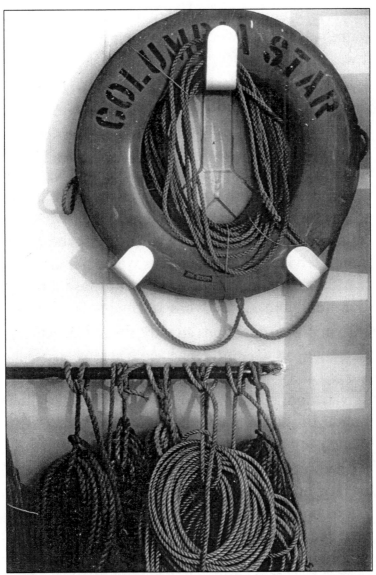

Columbia Star life ring and heaving lines, 1986. (From personal collection)

some social restrictions, occasional loneliness, but also lots of time to read, plenty of fresh air and blue water, and a good-sized paycheck every season when it was all over.

Judy, though understandably reluctant, agreed to support my new maritime plans. Her father having sailed as a fireman for most of her childhood, she knew what it was like to be apart for extended periods. We thought the breaks and eventual reunions would also add more sizzle to our relationship. Some of our most memorable moments when we were dating had been those times when I returned home from the boats. The tremendous welcome, the hugs and kisses, the long walks together. Those three or four month breaks had worked wonders.

To improve conditions slightly, the unions had implemented a sixty-thirty package whereby an officer worked sixty days on, then received thirty days off for vacation, all paid. With the addition of the three months off during the winter, it hardly compared to the nonstop pace of a retail business.

I had hit my thirties; reality was slapping me in the face, and I realized that it was time to make some tough choices. Though I tried to keep my life somewhat focused, chaos had a peculiar way of always blurring the lines. Sometimes, I wondered if my life would ever take off the way I'd hoped. Where was my big break? There had been so many detours, so many different directions that led nowhere in particular. My restlessness drove me to search for more satisfying things to do with my life; yet it all seemed so elusive. I needed a more meaningful purpose, something that would resonate. Perhaps, I was looking at things through rose-colored glasses; but at the time, my plan seemed flawless.

As the pieces of this puzzle came together, I would hopefully be making a smooth transition to a better way of life. For one thing, each year would have a foreseeable beginning and end, unlike the retail business. My wife and I would be able to spend more time with each other and actually be able to take a real worry-free vacation every year. This more comfortable lifestyle would allow me the opportunity during my time home to do more woodworking and perhaps create a few special furniture pieces for the house. With my degree in furniture design, I had been yearning to do this kind of work. It was a chance for me to explore more creative ideas without any great financial burden. Hadn't Maslow always encouraged us to climb another rung on his ladder?

Attending classes that first summer was a welcome change from working in the claustrophobic atmosphere of the local mall. Out on the blue waters of Grand Traverse Bay, we learned to row and command the double-ended lifeboats. Coordinating one's individual oar strokes with those of a dozen other cadets and trying to follow the orders of the coxswain were not the easiest skills to master. In fact, one afternoon

as we were rowing across the bay, somewhere between the "up oars" command and the signal to "give
way," one of the female cadets accidentally clubbed
me in the head with her wooden oar. When the stars
finally stopped spinning in my head, this cadet, by
the name of Barb, apologized profusely and practically called for a stretcher. For a few minutes, I was
groggy and disoriented, while Barb became Florence
Nightingale in all the confusion. In her concern for
my injury, she seemed to bubble with high energy
and a take-charge attitude. The lump on my head was
fine after a short while. We later joked about it and
became the best of friends. But I made sure to keep a
safe distance from her the next time we had lifeboat
drills. Why tempt fate?

To practice basic sailing skills, we paired up and pi-
loted our tiny Sunfish sailboats back and forth across
the bay. Some days, I had a hard time remembering
I was in school. On other occasions, we awkwardly
climbed into orange foam survival suits, "Gumby
suits" as they are called, and jumped off the pier into
deep water. Submerging for about five seconds, we
shot up to the surface like corks and clumsily swam
over to the waiting inflatable life raft. If the ship was
ever in imminent danger and we had to perform this
maneuver, we could only hope it would be a sunny
July day such as this. But, of course, we knew better. Murphy's Law would surely find a way to play
a role. However, the good thing about survival suits

was they definitely kept you warm and very buoyant, a great improvement over simple life jackets.

Attending class, all cadets were expected to wear uniforms that included khaki shirts and slacks, black shoes, and black ties. I suppose this dress code was an attempt to foster camaraderie and discipline. But it seemed more like unnecessary military regimentation. I sometimes felt like a boot camp recruit learning to answer to my superior officers. There was no need to treat us like buck privates. Besides, officers on the lakes tended to dress quite casually, rarely in any sort of uniform. Understandably, the term *academy* almost implies the wearing of uniforms. On the main campus, we stood out as maritime cadets. Still, I hadn't felt this self-conscious in a uniform since Boy Scout days in high school when our troop leader suggested that we wear our full regalia to class. No, I decided, not unless I wanted to get my ass kicked.

As the year progressed, we stayed quite busy in our classes. We slowly acquired such nautical skills as boxing the compass and distinguishing magnetic north from true north, as well as memorizing Morse code and endless Coast Guard regulations. We studied navigational rules of the road and various types of nautical chart projections. I was overwhelmed by the heavy cost of so many navigation textbooks and seamen's manuals. It didn't help much that my Bowditch's *American Practical Navigator*, my most expensive book, became an exciting chew toy for

Raleigh, my new cocker spaniel puppy. One lazy afternoon, having already dug up the backyard to bury countless bones, with nothing better to do, my innocent little puppy proceeded to shred the entire volume into a mushy pile of wet pulp. He looked pleased with his work though somewhat exhausted. I think he especially enjoyed the chapter on celestial navigation, so intriguing and yet challenging.

For weeks, we pored over Great Lakes charts, learning some of the more important aids to navigation, such as lighthouses, day beacons, flashing lights (red, green, and white), ranges, range lights, hazards to navigation, and so forth. The most interesting part of our training was learning to plot courses across the lakes. One had to take many factors into account for every course calculation, such as speed, distance to the next waypoint, as well as drift due to wind direction and current. This wealth of nautical information was a new stream for me to swim in, and I felt happily immersed. The academic life of a cadet was so different from the working life of a deckhand. It demanded considerably more responsibility and attention to detail. Of course, I had only scratched the surface. Later courses would teach us the layout and design of steam engines, as well as how a mate should properly load and unload a ship. We would learn how to guide a ship through the narrow confines of various river systems such as the St. Mary's, the St. Clair, and the Detroit River. Beyond this, we would also develop the essential skills of radar and marine radio communication.

With such a heavy load of information for the cadets to assimilate, we were well aware that the main purpose of this detailed and thorough instruction was to pass the Coast Guard examinations for our licenses. The instructors focused our attention on this mantra every other day. The exam was paramount. Yet, there were times when I questioned specific information on some of our classroom handouts. Information in our books seemed to differ from information we were being asked to memorize. Our instructors simply explained this by saying there was a correct answer and then there was the "Coast Guard" answer. As we later learned, third-year cadets who had recently taken the Coast Guard licensing exam were regularly asked to regurgitate as many of the questions and answers from the test as they could possibly remember. These answers were then used to help instruct the next group of test takers. Even if the answers were not "book" correct, they became the correct answers for the Coast Guard exam. I never understood this game and even questioned the instructors about it. But it was a catch-22 that we couldn't seem to do much about. They didn't want anyone to rock the boat and spoil the system.

One of the highlights of my time at the maritime academy was a visit one fall by Gordon Lightfoot. He had come to honor the 10-year anniversary of the sinking of the *Edmund Fitzgerald*. One of the academy deck cadets, David Weiss, was among those who had gone down with the ship in November of 1975. Laying a wreath upon Grand Traverse Bay, Lightfoot had come to pay tribute to the sailors who died in that tragedy. The song he wrote, "The Wreck of the Edmund Fitzgerald," was the finest honor he could have paid to those left behind. His music captured the essence of that fateful night and the eerie speculation that followed. I was fortunate to have been awarded the Gordon Lightfoot scholarship that fall, and I had a chance to meet him briefly at a reception and exchange a few words. He seemed genuinely concerned with the welfare of Great Lakes sailors and the precarious life they had chosen. All of the cadets felt very grateful for his generosity and thoughtfulness, for spending time with us in Traverse City on this solemn occasion. Lightfoot's song had stirred many powerful memories that would not soon fade.

Dead Reckoning

Dead reckoning: *noun* 1) the calculation of one's position, especially at sea, by estimating the direction and distances traveled, 2) calculation based on inference or guesswork

After the first year of training at the Maritime Academy, the school placed each of the cadets on a Great Lakes freighter for two and a half months to observe up close the work of mates and engineers. We were expected to complete an extensive written sea project during this time, as well as work with the officers. Catching the boat in Toledo in June, I joined the crew of the *Columbia Star,* a thousand-footer owned by the Oglebay Norton Company. I shared a room one deck below the bridge with another cadet from the academy who was working on his engineer's license. When I stepped aboard, I could hardly believe the tremendous size of the *Columbia Star*—more than three football fields long and over a hundred feet wide. It absolutely dwarfed the other ships I'd sailed on. This was the first time that I'd been on a vessel in which all the cabins were aft. To travel from the engine room to the pilothouse, there were a good many decks to climb.

The first mate asked that I stand watch in the pilothouse anytime we entered the rivers, the locks, or came into port. The rest of the time I could spend on my sea project. Whenever we approached the St Mary's River downbound at Gros Cap or upbound at Detour, or when we neared the St. Clair River or Detroit River on the lower lakes, my job was to be on the bridge observing and taking notes. When we locked through at the Soo, or came into port at Silver Bay, Duluth, or Toledo, I was in the pilothouse soaking up what I could.

Learning the rivers became quite a challenge. I had to tediously memorize all the courses and distances between waypoints throughout the river system. It was important to know where in the channel to start a turn, how slow or fast to take it, and what speed to run. The ship handled much differently, more sluggishly, when she was loaded with 63,000 tons of ore than when she was empty. Every course change the mate called out, the wheelsman repeated aloud before executing the turn. During a change of watch, I would sometimes walk into a pitch-black pilothouse, and all I could see were the lights along the river and the flashing buoys to guide us. It would take a few minutes for my eyes to adjust. Other freighters were approaching us upbound in the channel, and we steered to the right side to allow them clearance. The mate stressed that it was critical that I know exactly where we were in the river, day or night, whenever I entered the pilothouse. Ranges, buoys, beacons, flashing lights, everything had a purpose, and my job was to memorize it and use it. Between the sea project and memorizing courses, I stayed as busy as I wanted.

Slowly, after a number of weeks aboard the *Columbia Star,* my mind started to wander to other places, other possibilities. There were long periods in the pilothouse when nobody said a word. In dead silence, the mate and wheelsman just stared out at the water and the buoys, lost in a trance. In the rivers, the old man was perched on his stool on the port side, scanning the daily newspaper. Every few minutes, without looking up, he asked what speed we were making or whether we had checked in with the Coast Guard at the last waypoint. As hour after hour crawled by, we drifted silently down the river like a giant ice floe. The mate on watch stood in the front window directly ahead of the wheelsman. I stood in the window to his right, jotting down in my river book each new waypoint, the time, and the new course. The waypoint could be a spot in the river where the pilothouse was abeam of a factory smokestack or warehouse, some kind of landmark to indicate the turning point in the ship's course. Out on the lake, it could be a lighthouse or even an island. My watches were always spent standing, never sitting, sometimes for an eight-hour period.

Out on the open lake, other than the sea project, there was much less for a cadet to do. Life in the pilothouse had become so automated, so high tech, that the mate's priority was to simply monitor the different systems. The Loran-C system guided the ship across the lake effortlessly. We simply watched for course changes at the waypoints, monitored the weather on the radio, and calculated our new ETA (estimated time of arrival) at each point. Otherwise, we either made small talk or meditated all the way across the lake, merely putting in our time to get through the watch. Subjects ranged from the latest rumors and scuttlebutt on various crew members to what was happening to the steel industry. Again, my mind began to wander. I thought of being somewhere else, doing something more interesting, more gratifying, with this time. Was I here, I asked myself, for the money, for the challenge, for the change of pace, for the invigorating sea life? My dream of becoming a mate was slowly evaporating. The life of a lowly deckhand, by comparison, seemed to hold more appeal.

After a month's isolation on the boat, I decided to head up the street in Toledo one afternoon with a couple of the deckhands. I had made friends with them, and it was great to get away, tell some sea stories, and throw down a few beers. About eleven p.m., I arrived back at the dock and headed up to my room for a few winks. Judging the time it would take to cross Lake Erie and to approach the rivers, I figured I should be heading up to the pilothouse by two a.m. I didn't have an alarm clock, but I knew I could just wake up if I set my mind to it. Of course, I had no sooner dozed off than I was jolted awake by some inner alarm. I leapt to my feet, rubbed my weary beer-soaked eyes, and looked out my porthole. We had already passed the Detroit River Light, which was my cue to appear on the bridge. Figuring I was about five minutes late, I scrambled into my clothes, up the stairway, and into the darkened pilothouse. I mumbled my apologies for being late and quietly took my position to the right of the front window. For the next four hours, as we made our way up the Detroit River in the darkness, across Lake St. Clair, and through the St. Clair River, I tried to look focused. My head was pounding with a hangover, and I felt like I could fall asleep any minute standing up. Every few minutes, I lifted the binoculars that hung from my neck and peered ahead at the twinkling darkness. I tried my best to stay alert by identifying approaching ships and flashing buoys. But it was almost a lost cause. Waves of sleep were washing over me; I had to shake my head and shift from one foot to the other just to remain conscious. Several hours passed this way, and soon the morning sky was visible in the east. In the early light, the captain, the mate, the wheelsman, and I could now see one another very clearly. As we neared the Blue Water Bridge in Port Huron, which would signal the end of my watch, I was thankful that I hadn't dropped to the deck in my sleep-deprived hangover haze. Lifting my binoculars to locate buoys number one and two just north of the bridge, I stared vacantly out at the horizon, trying to kill a few more precious minutes. Soon I could disappear below and crawl into my cozy bunk. But as I stared through my binoculars, I slowly realized that I didn't actually have binoculars. I had been staring through my two cupped hands for God only knows how long; my real binoculars still hung from my neck. Not wanting to draw any attention my way, I dropped my hand binoculars to my side in slow motion and then carefully turned to see if anyone had caught my slight blunder. Thankfully, I had been invisible. We reached the two buoys and I retired. That was the last time I ever drank anything before a watch. Though good karma sometimes favored me, sheer stupidity was just around the corner.

One thing that nobody ever complained about on the *Columbia Star* was the food. The meals were tremendous. Steaks, chicken, fish, shrimp, chops—the cook was outstanding. The second cook proved to be his equal with his fresh pies, cookies, and pastries every morning. I had to cut back to two meals a day, but still it was hard to avoid the goodies. After awhile,

I was afraid to step on a scale. To compensate for my overindulgence, I began lifting weights, pedaling the stationary bicycle, and walking the deck regularly. If I didn't lose much weight, at least it soothed my guilty conscience.

As I was starting to get the hang of things, and making more friends with the other crew members, I decided one afternoon to explore downtown Duluth while the ship was loading. Departing with a few of the guys in a taxi, I noted that the ETD was 1630. We had four and a half hours to ourselves. What a joy it was just to walk through gift shops, bookstores, or any retail outlets. The stimulation from all the color and variety and gadgetry was overwhelming. I hadn't realized, until I lived on a ship, how accustomed we'd grown to the absence of everyday creature comforts, a sort of sensory deprivation. Most of the furnishings we lived with aboard ship were either steel or hard-surfaced—the cold steel stools in the crew's mess room, the steel chairs in our cabins, the steel decks we walked on. The cushiest part of the boat was the bunk I slept in. It felt so refreshing to walk freely about town, observing other people, or simply to visit the maritime museum out by the breakwall. I discovered an interesting book in one of the shops and, at a local tavern, settled down comfortably with a beer. As I listened to the jukebox and enjoyed my break from the ship, I casually glanced at my watch. There was still time for one more beer.

Phoning my wife back home, I told her I had to cut it short since the ship would be departing shortly, at four-thirty. It had been a leisurely afternoon, and I hated to end it. But I soon hailed a cab and headed back to the dock. As the taxi pulled up to the docks about four-fifteen, the *Columbia Star* had already thrown off her mooring cables and was under way about twenty feet off the dock. I hollered and waved frantically up to the mate on deck, but it was too late for the ship to turn back. In a panic, I thought I would have to catch a Greyhound bus and meet them in the Soo. But the taxi driver, having seen similar things happen before, suggested we drive out to the Duluth high bridge and try to hire a tugboat to ferry me out to my ship. We had no more than fifteen minutes time to make arrangements while the *Star* weaved her roundabout way out to the breakwall. The driver raced through the streets of Duluth and down to the aerial bridge dock and, at the same time, radioed the tugboat captain to be ready for a passenger in about ten minutes. Leaping aboard the tug, I donned my life jacket, and we raced out to the *Star* as she turned in the channel. The tugboat skipper had radioed ahead that I was coming aboard, and the engine room crew stood ready in the open gangway to grab me when I jumped. The tug couldn't get any closer than four or five feet from the gangway without striking the ship. With open arms waving, they hollered, "Jump! Jump! We'll catch you!" The tugboat was bouncing around, and the waves between the two vessels were churning from the propeller backwash. When the tug rose up on the crest of a wave, I leaped into a sea of arms that grabbed me and pulled me to safety. How ridiculous this entire situation seemed. I had simply lost track of time, and the ship had departed slightly ahead of the posted 1630 ETD. As soon as the boat was loaded, the captain quickly got under way; he waited for no one, certainly not a lowly cadet. What a bizarre finish to such a pleasant afternoon. One moment, a relaxing, carefree afternoon uptown; the next, a frantic race against time. With minor damage to my pride, I had at least saved face by finding a way to rejoin my ship. The Greyhound trip would have been asking too much.

By early August, I had nearly completed my sea project and had mailed all the paperwork back to the school. I had spent many hours working on my assignments, running from one end of the ship to the other searching for various tidbits of nautical information. I thought things would gradually fall into place if I gave them enough time. But my boredom grew, time dragged on, and I began dreaming of more rewarding things to do with my life. By late July, I began to earnestly question my career prospects on the Great Lakes. I had spent a fair amount of time and money pursuing this goal and had worked diligently in school, but the bottom line was that my heart was simply not in it anymore. I could have continued in school to obtain my mate's license, but my desire was vanishing. My ambition slowly became a delusion.

One reason for this shift was my realization and disappointment that new technology had replaced so many nautical skills. Because of these improvements in technology, navigation had become safer and more precise. An officer could now pinpoint his ship's location anywhere on the lakes within several feet. Many of his age-old, well-honed nautical skills were unneeded, unless the equipment suddenly broke down. But, at the same time, something was lost. There was a sense that men were no longer in complete control of this ship, but rather that machines had taken over. The deck officers had been reduced to caretakers and monitors. With the exception of river navigation knowledge, a large amount of a mate's skills had effectively been thrown on the scrap heap. I would prefer to have sailed a hundred years ago when those maritime skills were essential to navigate the lakes. Similarly, I would love to have been a cabinetmaker back in the early nineteenth century, a time when skilled artisans with hand tools plied their trades. However, the great majority of today's consumers don't rely on woodworkers or cabinetmakers to build their furniture; instead, they purchase mass-produced pieces made in large, impersonal factories. Maybe it's not worth lamenting the vanishing need for nautical skills anymore than the loss of handcrafted objects. Technology is both friend and foe; for many of our high-tech gains, we suffer a hands-on personal loss. Such progress is a double-edged sword.

Another cause of my dissatisfaction was my overwhelming sense that both officers and crew were simply putting in their time, numbering the days until the next vacation, holding on for nothing more than a good-paying job. Of course, there are people in many walks of life who are bored or unhappy with their chosen work. Some merely tolerate their jobs; they go about their work in a half-hearted spirit, somewhat disconnected. Obviously, we all need jobs to sustain ourselves; but why not take the time to find the right fit? We tend to underestimate our needs, accepting whatever comes along, when we should be holding out for more.

One might think that sailing on the wide-open Great Lakes would lend itself to a happy-go-lucky, freewheeling sort of lifestyle, an opportunity for priceless sunsets and panoramic moments. And in many ways, it truly did. But after a time, my perspective changed. I experienced an overpowering sense of confinement and isolation. Gradually, I realized that I wanted an environment that offered both spontaneity and freedom, that allowed for creative expression, that encouraged a sense of humor in daily life. By contrast, shipboard life for officers was loosely regimented; there were no uniforms or stripes, but there was a very definite pecking order. What was missing, for me, was more aesthetic participation in life. I missed simple things, like playing my guitar and my drums, learning the piano, as well as woodworking and stained glass. The books I had brought with me rescued me on many occasions. I missed laughing and telling stories with old friends. I missed holding my wife and being able to express my thoughts and feelings to her. It felt like all my personal relationships had been put on the back burner and were slowly evaporating. I had a need for more hands-on inspiration, for more aesthetic expression, for a means of celebrating life and what it means to be whole. Why did I have to come so far to understand what was missing from my life? More than anything, I felt compelled to express my own individualism. I had to find a life with more spirit and imagination.

For all practical purposes, the romance of sailing on the Great Lakes was fading fast; in hindsight, its appeal had been greatly exaggerated. From the shore, life on the freighters had always appeared more mysterious and alluring. But things had changed. At times, to remind myself, all I needed was to glance over at my roommate, another academy cadet. He would lie back on his bunk for hours smoking a cigarette, brooding about something, staring into the void. He dragged himself through each day like a prisoner in solitary, biding his time. Every week he counted exactly the number of days he'd been aboard and how many yet to go. Life, to him, seemed anything but sweet. He appeared to be alienated from himself and everyone around him. As the unwilling cell mate, I had to escape.

My wife and I were expecting our first baby in September. At first, I thought I could adjust to being away from my family, to a mate's life of coming and going throughout the year. But now I wanted our new baby to grow up with me in his life, to know me, to be able to ask me questions when the time came. I wanted the responsibilities and the joys of being a father, and I did not want to miss any of the growth or changes. My father had missed the better part of my growth as a child and teenager because he was stationed in the army at some distant location. I often wondered how different things might have been had he lived with us more while my siblings and I were growing up.

For many men and women, working on the lakes is a rewarding career. I have several friends who love the sailing life. One is a river pilot for foreign vessels on the Great Lakes; he guides them safely through the St. Mary's River system. Another is a chief engineer who travels the oceans to Europe, Asia, and the Mideast. Still another friend serves as a first mate on a Great Lakes thousand-footer. They are all very skilled at what they do and enjoy the challenge. Yet, our temperaments are quite different. I discovered that I don't particularly like taking orders and working under someone else. I prefer to make my own decisions and be responsible for them. I enjoy being a team player but find that I can accomplish more on an individual level, and with greater satisfaction. Once I became aware of my temperament, I knew I had to work for myself.

It came down to finding more balance in my life. I was trying to find the right connection, the spark that makes work worthwhile, that gives every day a purpose. Perhaps it's a perspective or an attitude or a sense of values. However elusive or transcendent, it was something worth pursuing. Thoreau recommended that we simplify our lives on a regular basis. Discard the clutter frequently. Keep the essentials and the things that matter most. Find the right balance. In so doing, each of us needs solitude as well as society; the proportions vary with the individual. I love privacy and quiet as much as parties and conversation. I've found that I can function better on my own than as part of a large group. For me, it's a balancing act that I must continually adjust.

Once again, I was weighing anchor and sailing for an unknown port. But this time the wind was with me. I had a sense that my course was true.

"Not until we are lost do we begin to understand ourselves."

---Henry David Thoreau

Homeward Bound

As an eighteen-year-old kid, a few seasons of sailing on the freighters was just the catalyst I needed to come to terms with some troubling issues. It was an opportunity for me to see life up close and to experience a way of living that was both invigorating and frustrating. With the perspective of time comes appreciation and understanding of events that, at the time, seemed like total chaos and confusion.

Working as a deckhand on the lakes taught me quite a bit about other people, but more about myself. I used to think that there was a reason for every good or bad thing that happened; that there was a right and a wrong solution to every problem; that everybody but me had a focused goal and knew exactly what they wanted out of life. I wondered how any high school graduate could have even the foggiest idea what he wanted to do for the rest of his life. And yet, many graduates did. At eighteen, they knew with certainty that they wanted to become lawyers, doctors, pharmacists, or teachers. I couldn't understand how they had arrived at such sure-footed confidence and assurance. I, on the other hand, was completely lost. Although I had some vague idea of the direction I wanted to pursue, I chose to go slowly, to explore all my options.

Most of the choices we make are not black and white; there will always be shades of gray. In order to make decisions, we need to unravel the complexities to a simpler, more understandable core. To move forward in life, we must often make difficult choices; we must not put them off and just sit on the fence post. Whenever I procrastinate, I seem to regret it later. In the long run, I find it wiser to gather as much information as I can about a problem, consider all the alternatives, and make an informed decision. I leave the second-guessing to someone else.

Working on the boats at a young age was a blessing in so many ways. I was fortunate to have sailed several years as a deckhand and to have served as a maritime cadet as well. Crossing paths with so many different crew members taught me how to get along with a wide variety of personalities. Some of the quirks and eccentricities seemed more pronounced aboard ship, perhaps because of the isolation and remoteness of living out on the lakes. Although it created a sense of loneliness at times, sailing presented me the chance to confront myself and the person I wanted to become, and ultimately, to appreciate many of the good things I had in my life. I had the time to

Sugar Islander II ferry, crossing the St. Mary's River at Little Rapids Cut. (From personal collection)

read, the time to think, and the time to make plans for the future.

Sailing on the freighters allowed me to experience a lifestyle that is changing, if not slowly vanishing. Like many other large American industries, the basic functions of a Great Lakes ship have been automated. Technology has greatly improved both the navigation and the engineering capabilities of today's vessels. Likewise, the labor force necessary to operate a ship has diminished from roughly thirty-two men and women to about twenty-two. Many job duties have been combined and can be performed by fewer crew members. Like any business, the bottom line is about cutting costs to stay competitive.

Seeing the Great Lakes in all their glory, in all

four seasons, was a priceless experience. It would be difficult to exaggerate the overall grandeur of the lakes, their unpredictable moods, their truly awesome beauty. Twain had his mighty Mississippi River and Melville his endless ocean; we have our Great Lakes. What a magnificent treasure.

In many ways, the hopes and dreams of my fellow crew members were no different than in any other walk of life. People everywhere want many of the same things: a sense of acceptance and belonging, camaraderie with fellow workers, a sense of purpose, and recognition for a job well done. It all comes down to finding a connection to our fellow human beings and the work that we do, no matter what type of work it is. There can be honor and meaning in the humblest of duties. What is important is for each one of us to discover what resonates for us individually. We all have passions that we must identify, nourish, and follow. In this way, we establish our individual connections to the world in a meaningful way.

Socrates once observed that "the unexamined life is not worth living." How can a person expect to grow personally and spiritually unless he takes time to reflect upon his own life? Searching for my own self-identity over the years has led me to a number of conclusions. To maintain my sanity, I need to balance myself between work and play. I enjoy hard work as long as I can temper it with some diversions. There are so many absurdities to life that it's impossible not

Irving S. Olds, near Mission Point in the Soo, early 1980s.
(Courtesy of the photographer, Fred Hill)

to laugh at them every day. I have a need for aesthetics in my life whether it's reading books, attending the theater, or jamming with other musicians. Some of my favorite times are when I'm sitting around with friends telling stories. We just never know what interesting tales might come out.

I have trouble with people who misuse their authority. Having seen it so often, I find it better to be my own employer and to steer clear of situations in which I am part of a pecking order. My temperament is better suited to making decisions by myself in a work setting and living with the consequences of those decisions, whether good or bad.

Some things never end. For me, the need to simplify the various parts of my life is a constant battle that I wage. Sorting out and getting rid of the clutter regularly makes daily life more manageable. If I neglect it, I am soon overwhelmed. Family life can easily grow complicated with so many different needs and schedules, but we try to sort it out and streamline it whenever possible. Multitasking is not necessarily something to be admired. Better to eliminate some of the less important jobs on the list and work on the remaining ones at a slower, more enjoyable pace.

Working on the boats gave me an appreciation for many of the things and people that I already had in my life. I try now to live in the present, not simply to plan for the future. There is so much that we miss if we overplan and don't allow for spontaneity.

For me, it is essential to find a sense of purpose in my work, to search for a path that offers both spirit and imagination, work that can lend joy to others. Jerome Segal, in *Graceful Simplicity,* (p. 99), speaks of the dignity that any calling must include: "A work life that denies our individuality, our creativity, or our moral and aesthetic sensibility is a work life that denies our dignity as human beings." It is important to always take pride in a job well done, no matter how simple, no matter how humble. These small satisfactions add up eventually and make any job worthwhile and more pleasurable.

My belief in the good karma-bad karma principle has strengthened. Basically, it is the belief that by doing good things in the world to help other living things, we create a positive energy that radiates like the ripples from a stone thrown in a pond. Many of the world's religions have a similar concept. The good that you do accumulates and may someday help you when you least expect it. Its essence is that helping others is a reward in itself.

Up to a point, I value technology for the way it has improved our lives. While I am fascinated by the new dimensions that my computer has opened up to me, I am also careful not to allow the machine to dominate my life. Computers, cell phones, DVDs, ipods, and other communication technologies can practically control our lives 24/7 if we allow them. If we buy into that, we agree to a faster-paced, more frantic style of living in which our leisure hours are soon taken up by myriad tidbits of information that we could easily do without. By using technology as a tool rather than as a crutch, we work towards greater independence and self-reliance.

As a former deckhand, I consider what cargoes are entrusted to my safekeeping and to what distant ports I am bound. I encourage others to sail to those ports that excite them and to find a cargo worth carrying. The journey can't begin until you set the course and let go the lines.

⚓ ⚓ ⚓

In the morning mist along the St. Mary's River, the *Columbia Star* glided by near Mission Point. The

Sugar Island ferry tied up at the island dock to await the freighter's passage. Overhead, the Canada geese stretched out in a flying wedge, the lead goose honking loudly to keep the others in formation. With early winter coming on, the last of the dry birch and maple leaves blew across the faded grass and scattered into the river. The freighter, bound for the lower lakes, faded around the bend in the river, slowly disappearing in the morning haze.

⚓ ⚓ ⚓

One hundred years from now, freighters will still ply these waters, hauling their cargoes from port to port. Ship designs may change, navigation and communication may improve considerably, but some things will likely remain the same. Somewhere on the lakes, among the crew of a giant ore freighter, some cranky bosun will be faced with the prospect of breaking in another new deckhand. With any luck, he'll have patience and a good sense of humor.

Nautical Terms Glossary

Abeam – 'On the beam', a relative bearing at right angles to the centerline of the ship's keel.

AB – Short for able seaman; experienced seaman in deck department, one grade higher than ordinary seaman (OS).

Aft – Towards the stern (of the vessel).

Aboard – On or in a vessel. *Close aboard* means near a ship.

Adrift – Afloat and unattached in any way to the shore or seabed. It may also imply that a vessel is not anchored and not under control, therefore goes where the wind and current take her, (Loose from moorings, or out of place).

Aground – Resting on or touching the ground or bottom.

Ahead – Forward of the bow.

Anchor – An object designed to prevent or slow the drift of a ship, attached to the ship by a line or chain; typically a

From *American Merchant Seaman's Manual, Sixth Edition,* William B. Hayler, Master Mariner, editor-in-chief; John M. Keever, Master Mariner, associate editor; Paul M. Seiler, Boatswain, associate editor; based on the original edition by Felix M. Cornell and Allan C. Hoffman; copyright 1938, 1940, 1942, 1946, 1957, 1981 by Cornell Maritime Press, Inc. Used with permission of Cornell Maritime press, Centreville, Maryland (800-638-7641)

Resource: Glossary of nautical terms, http://en.wikipedia.org/w/index. php?title=Glossary_of_nautical_terms&oldid=199349118 (last visited Mar. 28, 2008)

metal hook-like object designed to grip the bottom under the body of water.

Ashore – On the beach, shore or land.

Astern – Toward the stern; an object or vessel that is abaft another vessel or object.

Ballast – Water that is taken into a ship's side-or-bottom tanks to improve stability and trim.

Beacon – A lighted or unlighted fixed aid to navigation attached directly to the earth's surface. (Lights and day beacons both constitute beacons).

Bearing – The horizontal direction of a line of sight between two objects on the surface of the earth.

Belly – The distortion of the hull where the center is lower than the ends of the keel.

Berth – A bed on a boat, or a space in a port or harbour where a vessel can be tied up.

Bitter end – The anchor cable is tied to the bitts; when the cable is fully paid out, the bitter end has been reached. The last part of a rope or cable.

Bitts – Cast steel heads serving as posts to which cables are secured on a ship.

Boarding Ladder – The ladder which extends from the dock to the deck of a ship, used by crew and passengers to gain access to the vessel.

Boatswain or **Bosun** – Highest unlicensed rating on a ship; responsible for the deck crew and ship maintenance.

Bollard – Cast steel heads secured to a wharf or dock, and used for securing the lines from a ship. The bitts on a ship may also be called bollards.

Bosun's Chair – A hard plank seat attached to a heavy line, rigged on a boom and pulley, and used on Great Lakes freighters mostly to transfer deckhands to the dock.

Boxing The Compass – Naming the various graduations of the compass by using the point system; e.g., North, North by East, North Northeast, etc.

Buoy – A floating object of defined shape and color, which is anchored at a given position and serves as an aid to navigation.

Bowline – A type of knot, producing a strong loop of a fixed size, topologically similar to a sheet bend. Also a rope attached to the side of a sail to pull it towards the bow (for keeping the windward edge of the sail steady).

Bow – The front of a ship.

Bow Thruster – A small propeller located in a tunnel in the underwater hull of a ship, near the bow; improves maneuverability, especially when docking.

Breakwall (Breakwater) – A structure designed to protect a harbor from the effects of weather.

Bridge – Wheelhouse or pilothouse.

Bulkhead – An upright wall within the hull of a ship; particularly a load-bearing wall.

Bumboat – A private boat selling goods.

Chief Cook – A senior unlicensed crew member working in the ship's galley, whose duties include planning menus, preparing meals, taking inventory of stores and equipment, and directing galley personnel.

Chocks – Deck fittings for mooring line to pass through.

Cleat – A stationary device used to secure a rope aboard a vessel.

Coaming – The raised edge of a hatchway used to help keep out water.

Crew – All persons working onboard a ship.

Davits – Curved metal posts for lifting and lowering lifeboats at the ship's sides.

Dead Reckoning – The determination of position by advancing a known position for courses and distances.

Deckhand – A person whose job involves aiding the deck supervisor in (un)mooring, anchoring, maintenance, and general evolutions on deck.

Deckwatch – A member of the deck crew whose duties also include preparing the mooring lines for port, waking the next watch, and sounding the ballast tanks. The deckwatch works two 4-hour watches per day.

Downbound – Direction vessels are headed when they travel from Lake Superior or upper lakes area toward the St. Lawrence Seaway or lower Great Lakes ports.

Draft – The depth of a ship's keel below the waterline.

Eye – A small loop in the end of a line or cable.

Fantail – The overhanging stern section of a vessel, from the sternpost aft.

First Mate – The Second in command of a ship.

Fit-out – Period, usually in early spring, when the crew prepares the ship for another season; supplies of food, fuel, equipment, etc. are taken aboard.

Foreward – Toward the bow of the vessel.

Freeboard – The height of a ship's hull above the water line.

Front Window – The window in the pilothouse located directly in front of the wheelsman, and in line with the ship's steering pole, where the captain or mate often stands to direct the ship's course.

Galley – The kitchen of the ship.

Gunwale – (Gunnels) The upper edge of a boat's sides.

Hatches – Hatchway covers.

Hatch Farm – A lake freighter that uses large canvas tarps and battens to secure its hatches from the weather.

Hatchway – One of the large square openings in the deck of a ship through which freight is hoisted in or out, and access is had to the hold.

Harbor – A place where ships may find shelter from the weather or are stored. Harbors can be man-made or natural.

Hawse Pipe – A cast steel tube in the ship's bow through which the anchor chain passes.

Hawsepiper – An informal maritime industry term used to refer to a merchant ship's officer who began his or her career as an unlicensed merchant seaman and did not attend a traditional maritime college/academy to earn the officer license.

Head – The toilet or latrine of a vessel.

Headway – The forward motion of a boat.

Head Wire – Also known as bow line, this mooring line runs through chocks on the bow to a bollard on the dock; prevents backwards movement of the ship.

Heaving Line – A small and light line that is tied to a heavier mooring line for the purpose of passing it from ship to shore.

Hogging or **Hog** – The distortion of the hull where the ends of the keel are lower than the center.

Hold – A compartment for carrying cargo, below deck in a large vessel.

Holiday – A gap in the coverage of newly applied paint, slush, tar or other preservative.

Hulett Unloader – An electrically-operated, ore unloading machine with a large scoop bucket on one end; it can move along the dock to line up with various holds on an ore boat; used until about 1992, when self-unloading boats became standard.

Hull – The shell and framework of the basic flotation-oriented part of a ship.

Iron Deckhand – Another term for the hatch crane on a lake freighter, used to raise and lower the steel hatch covers on deck.

Keel – The central structural basis of the hull.

Knot – A unit of speed; one knot equals one nautical mile per hour.

Ladder – On board a ship, all "stairs" are called ladders, except for literal staircases aboard passenger ships. Most "stairs" on a ship are narrow and nearly vertical, hence the name.

Laker – Great Lakes slang for a vessel that spends all its time on the five Great Lakes.

Landing Boom – A long steel pole extending from a vertical post, along which a bosun's chair and line are rigged; used to lower deckhands to the dock to handle mooring lines.

Lay-up – The temporary cessation of trade by a ship no longer hauling cargo; period when a ship is tied up in port at the end of a shipping season or due to lack of business.

Lee side – The side of a ship sheltered from the wind (cf. weather side).

Leeward – In the direction that the wind is blowing towards.

Lifeboat – A small steel or wood boat located near the stern of a vessel. Used to get the crew to safety if something happens to the mothership.

Line – The correct nautical term for the majority of the cordage or "ropes" used on a vessel.

List – The vessel's angle of lean or tilt to one side, in the direction called roll.

Loran-C System – (Long Range Aid to Navigation) A technology used to establish a ship's position by measuring the time difference in the arrival of signals from two Loran stations.

Magnetic North – The direction in which a compass needle points; not the same direction as true north; the north geographic pole where the Earth's magnetic field is most intense.

Mates – Deck officers who assist the captain; on a Great Lakes freighter, there is usually a first mate, second mate, and third mate.

Navigation – The science of plotting and directing the course of a ship.

Navigation Rules – Rules of the road that provide guidance on how to avoid collision and also used to assign blame when a collision does occur.

Oiler – An unlicensed engine room member who oils and greases bearings and moving engine parts.

Ore Boat – Great Lakes term for a vessel primarily used in the transport of iron ore.

Pilothouse – Bridge or wheelhouse.

Port – Towards the left-hand side of the ship facing forward (formerly Larboard). Denoted with a red light at night.

Porter – Working in the galley, a porter helps prepare and serve meals to crew members; also helps clean and maintain officers' quarters; keeps galley and messroom clean and sanitary.

Porthole – A small round opening in the ship's shell plating.

Radar – Acronym for RAdio Detection And Ranging. An electronic system designed to transmit radio signals and receive reflected images of those signals from a "target" in order to determine the bearing and distance to the "target".

Range Lights – Two lights associated to form a range (a line formed by the extension of a line connecting two charted points) which often, but not necessarily, indicates the channel centerline. The front range light is the lower of the two, and nearer to the mariner using the range. The rear light is higher and further from the mariner.

Rudder – A swinging flat frame hung to the sternpost of a ship, by which the ship is steered.

Saltie – Great Lakes term for a vessel that sails the oceans.

Scuppers – An opening on the side rail that allows water to run off the deck.

Scuttlebutt – Shipboard rumors and gossip.

Seaman – Generic term for sailor, or (part of) a low naval rank.

Second Cook – Galley crew member who participates in the preparation and serving of meals; helps keep inventory of stores and equipment; often responsible for baking bread, rolls, cakes, pies, and pastries.

Self-Unloader – Great Lakes slang term for a vessel with a conveyor or some other method of unloading the cargo without shoreside equipment.

Ship's Bell – Striking the ship's bell is the traditional method of marking time and regulating the crew's watches.

Shoal – Shallow water that is a hazard to navigation.

Slip Knot – A knot which attaches a line to an object and tightens when tension is applied to the free end of the line; can be quickly undone by pulling the end of the loop.

Sougee – A very caustic, powdered cleaning agent used to scrub down the exterior cabin walls and bulkheads; often applied with long-handled brushes.

Sounding Rod – A round steel rod that is used to measure water depth in ballast tanks.

Splice – To join lines (ropes, cables, etc.) by unravelling their ends and intertwining them to form a continuous line. To form an eye or a knot by splicing.

Stanchion – An iron post or pillar for supporting the decks.

Starboard – Towards the right-hand side of a vessel facing forward. Denoted with a green light at night.

Stern – The rear part of a ship, technically defined as the area built up over the sternpost, extending upwards from the counter to the taffrail.

Stern Line – Mooring line from ship's stern to a dock bollard; leads well up the dock to prevent forward movement of the ship.

Straight Decker – A ship built with its pilothouse forward and engines aft to provide a continuous hold between.

Taconite – An iron ore product carried by many freighters on the Great Lakes, baked into a round pellet form, about one centimeter in diameter.

True North – A navigational term referring to the direction of the North Pole relative to the navigator's position.

Under way – A vessel that is not at anchor, or made fast to the shore, or aground.

Upbound – Term used to describe vessels headed from the St. Lawrence Seaway or lower Great Lakes toward Lake Superior or the upper lakes area.

Wake – Turbulence behind a ship.

Watch – A period of time during which a part of the crew is on duty. Changes of watch are marked by strokes on the ship's bell.

Watchman – An AB-rated seaman whose duties include relieving the wheelsman and standing lookout on the bow. The watchman also operates the winches when the ship is loading or locking through the Soo Locks.

Waypoint – A set of coordinates that identify a point in physical space; coordinates usually include latitude and longitude; waypoints have become widespread for navigational use since development of the Global Positioning System (GPS).

Wheelhouse – Location on a ship where the steering wheel is located, often interchanged with pilothouse and bridge.

Wheelsman – Crew member who steers the ship from the bridge, according to the commands of the captain or the mate on watch.

Whipping – Cord or twine wound around the end of a rope to keep it from fraying or unraveling.

Winch – A mechanical device (steam-powered or electric) used to wind up the steel mooring cables on a large spool or drum; may include a mechanical brake or ratchet that prevents it from unwinding.

Windlass – A winch mechanism, usually with a horizontal axis. Used where mechanical advantage greater than that obtainable by block and tackle was needed (such as raising the anchor on small ships).

Windward – In the direction that the wind is coming from.

Wiper – The most junior crew member in the engine room of a ship, whose job consists of wiping down machinery and keeping it clean.

Z-Card – (MMD) Merchant Marine Document issued by the U.S. Coast Guard; required of all crew members of U.S. ships with a gross register tonnage of over 100; allows one to work on the deck as an ordinary seaman (OS), in the engine department as a wiper, or in the galley as a porter.

About the Author

Rich is a recent escapee from the retail sector, having run both a gift store and a ready-to-finish furniture business. As an answer to holding a long-term mortgage, he continues to work on his owner-built log home (now approaching 15 years) with no obvious end in sight. Living on the upper St. Mary's River in Michigan's eastern Upper Peninsula, Rich spends much of his time reading and writing poetry and short stories. He is a grateful member of the Upper Peninsula Publishers and Authors Association (UPPAA). He also enjoys amateur photography, kayaking, brewing beer, and chasing after his wife, two boys, and their dog, Max. As an inveterate journal keeper, he has found a sure-fire way of warding off short-term memory lapses as well as a ready resource for many writing ideas.

Quick Order Form

Email orders: GaleForcePress.com

Postal orders: Gale Force Press, P.O. Box 374, Sault Ste. Marie, MI 49783-0374, USA; We accept personal checks, money orders, VISA, Mastercard, and Discover.

VISA, MC, DISCOVER # _____

Expiration Date _____ / _____ .

Enter the check code __ __ __ *(last 3 numbers on the back of credit card)*

Please send the following book(s):

Title	Price	Quantity	Total
Lake Effect	$17.95	_____	_____

Shipping & Handling _____

(Please add 6% for books shipped to Michigan addresses) Sales Tax _____

Total _____

Shipping:
U.S.: Add $4.00 for first book and $2.00 for each additional book
International: Add $9.00 for first book and $5.00 for each additional book.

Name: _____

Address: _____

City: _____ State: _____ Zip: _____

Telephone: _____

Email Address: _____

Special autograph instructions, if any: _____

Quick Order Form

Email orders: GaleForcePress.com

Postal orders: Gale Force Press, P.O. Box 374, Sault Ste. Marie, MI 49783-0374, USA; We accept personal checks, money orders, VISA, Mastercard, and Discover.

VISA, MC, DISCOVER # _____

Expiration Date _____ / _____ .

Enter the check code __ __ __ *(last 3 numbers on the back of credit card)*

Please send the following book(s):

<u>Title</u>	<u>Price</u>	<u>Quantity</u>	<u>Total</u>
Lake Effect	**$17.95**	_____	_____

Shipping & Handling _____

(Please add 6% for books shipped to Michigan addresses)   **Sales Tax** _____

Total _____

Shipping:

U.S.: Add $4.00 for first book and $2.00 for each additional book
International: Add $9.00 for first book and $5.00 for each additional book.

Name: _____

Address: _____

City:_____ State:_____ Zip:_____

Telephone:_____

Email Address: _____

Special autograph instructions, if any: _____

_____

Quick Order Form

Email orders: GaleForcePress.com

Postal orders: Gale Force Press, P.O. Box 374, Sault Ste. Marie, MI 49783-0374, USA; We accept personal checks, money orders, VISA, Mastercard, and Discover.

VISA, MC, DISCOVER # _____

Expiration Date _____ / _____ .

Enter the check code __ __ __ *(last 3 numbers on the back of credit card)*

Please send the following book(s):

<u>Title</u>	<u>Price</u>	<u>Quantity</u>	<u>Total</u>
Lake Effect	**$17.95**	_____	_____

Shipping & Handling _____

(Please add 6% for books shipped to Michigan addresses) **Sales Tax** _____

Total _____

Shipping:

U.S.: Add $4.00 for first book and $2.00 for each additional book
International: Add $9.00 for first book and $5.00 for each additional book.

Name: _____

Address: _____

City:_____ State:_____ Zip:_____

Telephone:_____

Email Address: _____

Special autograph instructions, if any: _____

_____

CPSIA information can be obtained at www.ICGtesting.com
Printed in the USA
BVOW03s1254230114

342763BV00005B/9/P